Religion and Ceremonies of the Lenape

The Delaware Native Americans, their History and Cultural Traditions

By M. R. Harrington

Published by Pantianos Classics

ISBN-13: 978-1-78987-355-9

First published in 1921

Contents

Conclusion of Lenape Annual Ceremony in Oklahoma.

Native Painting by Ernest Spybuck, a Shawnee (Frontispiece)

Preface

The following paper is intended to be the first of a series concerning different phases of the culture of the Lenape or Delaware Indians, once a numerous people forming a confederacy of three closely related tribes, the Unami, the Minsi or Muncey, and the Unala"tko or Unalachtigo, first encountered by the whites in what is now New Jersey, Delaware, eastern Pennsylvania, and southeastern New York, but at last accounts [1] reduced to some 1900 souls scattered in Oklahoma and the Province of Ontario, Canada, with a few in Wisconsin and Kansas. Of these the Lenape of Oklahoma seem to be mainly of Unami extraction, the rest largely Minsi, while the Unala"tko appear to have merged with the others and to have lost their identity.

The writer has gathered most of his data for the whole series from the Oklahoma bands, with such informants as Chief Charley Elkhair (Kokŭlŭpo'w"e), Julius Fox, or Fouts (Peta'nĭhink), Minnie Fox (Wemĕĕle'xkwĕ) his wife, and William Brown; but much valuable information came from Canada where his principal informants were Chief James Wolf ('Tayeno'xwan), Chief Nellis F. Timothy, (Tomapemihi'lat), Isaac Monture (Ka'pyŭ'hŭm), Chief Nellis Monture, Michael Anthony (Na'nkŭma'oxa), and Monroe Pheasant. Of these especial credit is due to Julius Fox and Chief Timothy, both of whom manifested great interest in the work and exerted every effort to make it complete, and to Ernest Spybuck, a Shawnee, whose paintings, carefully made of Delaware ceremonies at the writer's request, form a valuable adjunct to the text.

The works of previous writers have been utilized where available, and much has been learned from archeological discoveries in the ancient territory of the Lenape, not so much, of course, with regard to the subject matter of the present paper, as of others in preparation.

Most of the information was gathered while the writer was collecting ethnological specimens for the Heye Museum of New York, now the Museum of the American Indian, Heye Foundation, during the years 1907 to 1910; but some of the Canadian data were procured earlier while in the field for Mr. E. T. Tefft of New York, whose collection is now in the American Museum of Natural History.

Without knowledge of the Delaware language in its divergent dialects, and without any pretension of being a philologist, the writer has endeavored to record the Lenape words as he heard them, depending for translation on his interpreter *pro tem*. Hence some inaccuracies at least are inevitable. The alphabet used is as follows:

VOWELS

a as in arch.
ä as in cat.
â as in fall.
ai as in aisle.
e like a in fate.
ĕ as in met.
i as in machine,
ĭ as in hit.
o as in note.
u as in flute.
ŭ as in but.
û as in full.

CONSONANTS

c like English sh.
' a slight aspirate.
n gives the preceding vowel a nasal sound.

w faintly whispered.
L a surd l.
x like German ch.
Other consonants approximately as in English.

It was intended at first to publish the mass of material thus obtained in the form of a monograph on the ethnology of the Lenape; but later it was seen that while, some phases of their culture could be described in considerable detail, there were others not so well represented in our notes. It was therefore finally decided to publish at once such parts as were ready, in the form of separate papers, and to leave the others until more detailed information could be obtained.

No extended comparisons of the religion and ceremonies of the Lenape with those of other tribes will be attempted in this paper, these being reserved for a projected article to embody the results of a comparative study of Lenape culture.

M. R. Harrington

Chapter One - Pantheon

O the mind of the Lenape, all the phenomena of nature, all the affairs of mankind, in fact the entire world as we know it, is under the control of invisible beings. Some are great and powerful, others of somewhat lesser influence, and so on down to the humble spirits of plants and stones. In some, good seems to predominate, in others, evil; but most of the *manĭ'towuk*, or spirits, seem to be, like mortals, a mixture of desirable and undesirable qualities.

Supreme Being

All the Lenape so far questioned, whether followers of the native or of the Christian religion, unite in saying that their people have always believed in a chief *Manĭ'to,* a leader of all the gods, in short, in a Great Spirit or Supreme Being, the other *manĭ'towuk* for the greater part being merely agents appointed by him. His name, according to present Unami usage, is *Gicelĕmû'kaong',* usually translated, "great spirit," but meaning literally, "creator." Directly, or through the *manĭ'towuk* his agents, he created the earth and everything in it, and gave to the Lenape all they possessed, "the trees, the waters, the fire that springs from flint, — everything." To him the people pray in their greatest ceremonies, and give thanks for the benefits he has given them. Most of their direct worship, however, is addressed to the *manĭ'towuk* his agents, to whom he has given charge of the elements, and with whom the people feel they have a closer personal relation, as their 'actions are seen in every sunrise and thunderstorm, and felt in every wind that blows across woodland and prairie. Moreover, as the Creator lives in the twelfth or highest heaven above the earth, it takes twelve shouts or cries to reach his ear. An account of the worship of the Creator will be given later in connection with the description of the Annual Ceremony. The Minsi had similar beliefs, but the current name for the Great Spirit in that dialect today is *Pa''tŭmawas,* interpreted "He who is petitioned," or *Kĕ''tanĭto'wĕt,* "Great Spirit."

It has been frequently stated that the concept of a supreme being or chief of the gods was not known among the American tribes in pre-colonial times, and that the "Great Spirit" concept, now widely distributed among the Indians, is entirely the result of missionary teaching. This seems to have been the case in some instances, but it is a mistake to assume such a broad statement as a general rule, on *a priori* grounds. To the Indian mind, the spirits or gods partook largely of the nature of mankind — Why could not a chief of gods be as natural a concept as a chief of men? In the case of the Shawnee, the Creator or Great Spirit is usually spoken of as a woman, "Our Grandmother Paboth'kwe" — surely not a missionary idea!

Let us trace back the Great Spirit concept among the Lenape, and find what the early writers say about it. Perhaps the earliest is in Danker and Sluyter's Journal [2] of about 1679, in which an old Indian living near Bergen, New Jersey, is quoted as saying: "The first and great beginning of all things, was Kickeron or Kickerom, who is the origin of all, who has not only once produced or made all things, but produces every day. ...He governs all things."

William Penn, [3] in a letter dated Philadelphia, August 16, 1683, says: "They believe a God and Immortality; for they say, There is a King that made them, who dwells in a glorious country to the Southward of them, and that the Souls of the Good shall go thither, where they shall live again." Further confirmation is given by Holm [4] in his book first published in 1702, where he says, "They acknowledge a Supreme Being, a Great Spirit, who made the heavens and the earth."

Zeisberger [5] makes it even stronger, for he wrote, about 1779: "They believe and have from time immemorial believed that there is an Almighty Being who has created heaven and earth and man and all things else. This they have learned from their ancestors." Heckewelder [6] (p. 205) adds more details in his book, originally published in 1818: "Their Almighty Creator is always before their eyes on all important occasions. They feel and acknowledge his supreme power...It is a part of their religious belief that there are inferior *Mannittōs,* to whom the great and good Being has given command over the elements."

Finally, in the little work ostensibly dictated by the Minsi John Wampum, [7] known as Chief Waubuno, undated, but probably printed in the last quarter of the nineteenth century, we have "The Great Spirit, whom we call in Munsee or Delaware Kaunzhe Pah-tum-owans or Kacheh Munitto (Great Spirit or Benevolent Spirit), created the Indians."

Thus we have a practically unbroken chain of authorities, including most of the best ones since 1679, all speaking of the "Great Spirit" as a well-developed concept. But Brainerd, [8] writing in 1745, is not so positive in his statements, for he speaks of their notions being "so dark and confused, that they seemed not to know what they thought themselves." He also says: "Before the coming of the white people, some supposed there were *four* invisible powers, who presided over the *four* corners of the earth. Others imagined the *sun* to be the *only* deity, and that all things were made by him. Others at the same time have a confused notion of a certain *body* or *fountain* of deity, something like the *anima mundi.*" Later (p. 349) he quotes a converted Indian conjurer, who, in describing the

9

a   *b*

Lenape man and woman of Oklahoma in ceremonial costume

a, John Anderson (Witanaxkóxw'ĕ); *b*, Mrs Elkhair (Kicilungonĕ'xkwĕ) (Plate I.)

source of his former power, tells how it came from "a great man" who lived in a "world above at a vast distance from this. The great man was clothed with the day; yea, with the brightest day he ever saw...this whole world...was drawn upon him, so that *in* him, the earth, and all things on it, might be seen."

Perhaps, as Brinton [9] suggests, the original Great Spirit of the Lenape might really be called the God of Light. Brinton, however, does not think that this Spirit of Light was of necessity a good spirit; still, the Lenape today who follow the native religion, acknowledging his goodness in their ceremonies, think that "the Creator wants them to do right," and there is evidence [10] that the idea of goodness has been associated with that of the Great Spirit for a long time. Assuming that the Creator of the Lenape is the God of Light, what is it that leads men to worship the source of light? Is it not the self-evident benefits connected with light? It seems to the writer that goodness necessarily follows as an attribute of such a deity.

Evil Spirit

The case is different with the Evil Spirit. The modern Lenape in Oklahoma make little mention of an Evil One, and James Wolf, my principal Minsi informant, did not speak of such a being at all, but there is some evidence, however, to show this belief to exist among the Lenape in more recent years.

Some writers do indeed make frequent mention of "the Devil" as figuring in early Lenape belief, but they translate the word "manǐ'to" as having that meaning, whereas it really signifies a supernatural being, good or bad. These writers evidently regarded as "the Devil" any deity not fitting into Christian doctrine.

But the real truth seems to be that, while in ancient times certain *manǐ'towŭk,* or spirits, were supposed to work evil, the Devil (along with whiskey and other blessings) was introduced by the whites. The whole matter is well summed up by Loskiel [11] where he says: "Besides the Supreme Being, they believe in good and evil spirits, considering them as subordinate deities...They seem to have had no idea of the Devil, as the Prince of Darkness, before the Europeans came into the country." This idea is also supported by Zeisberger [12] and Brainerd, [13] although Holm [14] seems to give contrary evidence.

Manǐ'towŭk of the Four Directions

The Lenape now in Oklahoma believe that when the earth was created, and everything finished, the Creator gave the four quarters of the earth to four powerful beings, or *manǐ'towŭk,* whose duty it was to take care of these regions. These personages are the cause of the winds which blow from the different directions, with the exception of the tornado, which is thought to have a different origin. In the winter, it is said that the *manǐ'towŭk* of the north and the south are playing the game of bowl and dice, with alternating fortunes. When the north wind is successful it is cold for a long time, until the south wind wins again. These *manǐ'towŭk* are called *Moxhomsa' Wähänjio'pŭng,* Grandfather at the East; *No"oma Cawane'yŭng',* Grandmother at the South; *Moxhomsa' Eliosi' gak,* Grandfa-

11

ther at the West; and *Moxhomsa' Lowane' 'yŭng'*, Grandfather at the North, the expression *endalŭn towi'yŭn,* said to mean "who has charge of it" being frequently added after the name.

These are mentioned in the ritual of the Annual Ceremony, and the people often pray to them when gathering herbs or preparing medicines, at the same time offering tobacco.

The earliest record of this belief thus far found dates from 1616, and while it does not concern the Lenape proper, it illustrates a similar notion among a cognate people in Virginia. This is in Strachey's work, [15] in which he states, "The other four [gods] have no visible shape, but are indeed the four winds, which keep the four corners of the earth." Brainerd [16] mentions the same belief as being an old one among the Indians he knew, who were mainly Lenape, and as this was in 1745 we have at least a respectable antiquity established for "Our Grandparents at the Four Directions." Loskiel also mentions them. [17]

The Sun

To the Sun the Creator gave the duty of providing light for the people. The Unami say that he is a very powerful *manĭ'to,* and call him *Gĭckokwi'ta.* They speak of him as always clothed in the finest of deerskin garments, with his face handsomely painted, and wearing red feathers in his hair. Every day he travels across the heavens from east to west, stopping for a little while at midday, then going on. At night he comes back under the earth. The Minsi, according to James Wolf, called him *Ki'zho* or *Ki'zhox,* and *Gickonĭki'zho* is another Unami form of the name. When praying to the Sun, the Lenape usually addressed him as "Elder Brother."

Little is found in early writings concerning the worship of the Sun, a mere mention in Brainerd, [18] and Loskiel, [19] by whom he is called "the sun or the god of the day."

The Moon

None of my Lenape informants had much to say of the Moon, except that it was regarded as the *manĭ'to* charged with the duty of supplying light by night, and that it was addressed, like the Sun, as Elder Brother. It is mentioned as a god, and called the "night sun" by Loskiel. [20] This is expressed by the Unami name *Piske'weniki'zho.*

The Earth

Some Lenape speak of the earth itself as a *manĭ'to,* and call it "Our Mother" because it carries and nurtures the people, having been assigned that duty by the Creator. Others, instead of the earth itself, mention a spirit beneath or within the earth, but apparently separate from it. The earth is mentioned in a list of gods by Loskiel. [21] In some localities, at least, it was addressed in the Annual Ceremony, and thanks were offered to it for the benefits it gives to man.

Thunder Beings

Perhaps the most important of all the subordinate *manǐ'towŭk*, excepting only the Sun and possibly the Keepers of the Four Directions, were the Thunder Beings, to whom the Great Spirit gave the duty of watering the earth and protecting the people against Great Horned Water-serpents and other monsters. The Unami told me that they are called *Pethako-we'yŭk, and* are addressed as Elder Brother. They are man-like beings with wings, and always carry a bow and arrows with which they can shatter trees. When the first thunder is heard in spring, the people say, "The Spring Flying Things are coming" and it makes them feel glad to think that winter is nearly over. Some burn tobacco and pray to the Thunders at this and other times, and for this reason they claim that the lightning never used to strike an Indian or to destroy Indian property.

The late James Wolf related an interesting Thunder myth, which will be found in the paper on Lenape Mythology to appear later, stating that the Minsi called the Thunders *Pile'swak,* or *Pile'soak,* and believed them to exist in the form of gigantic partridges, although really persons, or rather *manǐ'towŭk.* They used to live in Niagara gorge beneath the cataract, and could sometimes be seen coming out, in the form of a cloud, in which, as it rose, a play of lightning was visible. There were said to be three bands or parties of these mysterious beings, each band consisting of three Thunders.

Zeisberger [22] says, "Thunder is a mighty spirit dwelling in the mountains," and Heckewelder, [23] "Indians, at the approach of a storm or thunder gust, address the Mannitto of the air, to avert all danger from them." As a rule, however, the early writers do not seem to have noticed this belief, or have included it loosely under the worship of "gods" representing the elements.

Keepers of the Heavens

The Lenape now in Oklahoma believe that each of the twelve heavens, in the highest of which lives the Great Spirit, is presided over by a *manǐ'to* who serves as a messenger to repeat the prayers of men until they reach the ear of the Creator. They are represented by the carved faces upon the posts inside the temple, and are mentioned in the ritual of the Annual

13

Ceremony. I can find no mention of them in early accounts of the Lenape, however, unless the twelve gods mentioned by Loskiel, [24] most of whom have already been spoken of in this chapter, may represent the same concept. The Lenape today speak of these as being related to the Living Solid Face, who will now claim our attention.

Fig. 1. — Mask of the Oklahoma Lenape. (Height, 14.5 in.)

Mĭsinghâli'kŭn, or Living Solid Face

The most remarkable deity of the Lenape is the Mask Being, called by the Unami *Mĭsinghâli'kŭn*, which was interpreted as "Living Mask," or "Living Solid Face." According to the Unami, this being was made guardian by the Creator of all the wild animals of the forest, and is sometimes seen riding about on the back of a buck, herding the deer; but he lives in a range of rocky mountains above the earth. His face is large and round, the right half being painted red, the left black, while his body is covered with long dark hair like that of a bear. Unlike most of the deities in the Lenape pantheon, he is represented by a "graven image, "a huge wooden mask, painted half red and half black (fig. i); which is left in charge of some family who will take good care of it, and burn Indian tobacco for it from time to time. With the mask is kept a coat and leggings of bearskin to represent the being's hairy body, a peculiar rattle of turtle-shell (fig. 2), a stick, and a bag made of bear-skin, all used by the man selected to imper-

14

sonate Mĭsinghâli'kŭn at the various ceremonies when he is supposed to appear, and which will be described later. To the back of the mask is fastened the skin of the bear's head, which effectually conceals the head and neck of the impersonator (pi. 11), while the bear's ears, projecting, add to the uncanny effect.

If any Lenape had a child who was weak, sickly, or disobedient, he would send word to the keeper of the mask that he wanted Mĭsinghâli'kŭn to "attend his child." It is said that it did not take the impersonator long to frighten the weakness, sickness, or laziness out of the child, so that thenceforth it would be strong and well, and would obey on the instant when asked to do anything. This effect was probably strengthened by the mother saying, "If you don't behave, Mĭsi'ngwʻ will carry you off in a bag full of snakes!" This seems to be the only trace of the doctoring function of the mask among the Unami. They also say that when the keeper burns tobacco for Mĭsinghâli'kŭn and asks for good luck in hunting, "it turns out that way every time;" and if anyone has

Fig. 2.— Rattle of turtle-shell used by Misi'ngʻ". (Length, 16.7 in.)

lost either horses or cattle, whether by straying away or through theft, he can go to the keeper of the Mĭsi'ngwʻ with some tobacco and recover them. All he has to do is to explain his errand to the keeper, who in turn informs Mĭsinghâli'kŭn that they want him to look for these particular animals. The loser then goes home, and in a few days the missing stock return, driven back by this mysterious being. If they were tied or hobbled, it is said that the Mĭsi'ngwʻ appears to them and so frightens them that they break loose and come home. Mĭsinghâli'kŭn has a special ceremony, held in the spring, and also participates in the Annual Ceremony at the Big House. This Mĭsi'ngwʻ is also called *Weopĕ'lakis,* to distinguish it from another, kept by a different family, which was not so important, and about which little was known by my informants except that, within their memories, it had never appeared at the Annual Ceremony, but that it probably had a spring dance of its own. There is an indistinct tradition, however, that in former times several masks were seen at the Annual Ceremony, and that half a day was given up to them.

Miniature masks (fig. 3) were often worn on the person as health or good-luck charms, in former days usually suspended from a string about the neck, but in later times carried in the pocket. The two large Unami masks in the Museum of the American Indian, Heye Foundation, are shown in pi. 11 and fig. 1.

15

Costume Worn By Impersonator of Misinghali'kun (Plate II.)

Among the Minsi there are considerable differences in belief and in practice, their masks resembling those of the Iroquois .in many particulars. The late James Wolf said that "Mĭsinghâli'kŭn" was supposed to live among the rocks on a hill, where he was first seen, and told the people how to obtain his power. The mask owners formed a society, which had a special meeting-house and ceremonies, and whose chief function it was to expell disease. This will be discussed further in another paper. Peter Jones [25] illustrates two Minsi masks in use in the first part of the nineteenth century, and these are here reproduced (pi. III). The first he calls a "Muncey idol," and says that it was "delivered up by Joe Nicholas on his

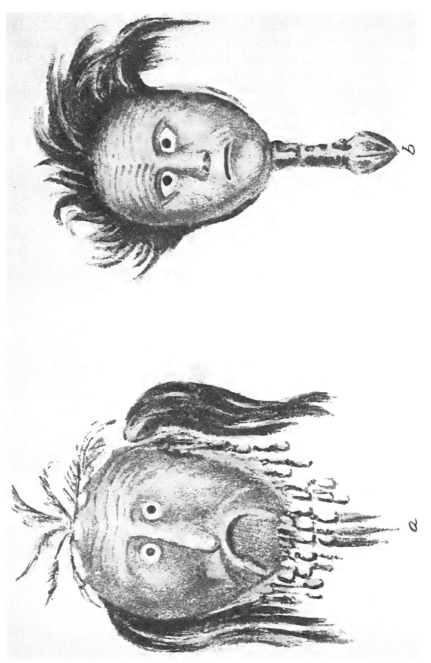

Masks of the Minisi (After Peter Jones) (Plate III.)

Conversion to Christianity," and that "Me Zeengk is the name of this God"; while the second, which he names "a Muncey devil idol," "formerly belonging to the Logan family," was "delivered up on the 26th of Jan. 1842."

17

Jones does not refer to these "idols" in the text. The second mask illustrated seems to have a turtleshell rattle tied on its back, the handle projecting downward. Another mask, found by the writer among the Lenape at Grand river, Ontario, and apparently of Minsi type, is shown in fig. 4. It was collected for Mr E. T. Tefft, of New York, but is now in the American Museum of Natural History.

Fig. 3. — Charm representing Mĭsinghâli'kŭn. (Height, 1.9 in.)

Some of our best evidence indicating the early existence of belief in this Mask Being among the Lenape is furnished by archeology — by the finding of a number of heads or masks of stone (pi. iv) within the boundaries of their former domain in New Jersey and the vicinity, [26] which, when the rarity of such objects in the surrounding regions is also considered, seems quite significant. Such stone heads even mark the trail of the Lenape withdrawal westward through Pennsylvania, [27] and have even been found in Ohio, where they lingered for a time (fig. 5).

The best early description is given by Brainerd, [28] who, in May 1745, while on the Susquehanna above the English settlements, saw a masked Indian who must have been an impersonator of Mĭsinghâli'kŭn. It runs:

"But of all the sights I saw among them, or indeed anywhere else, none appeared so frightful...as the appearance of one who was a devout and zealous Reformer, or rather, restorer of what he supposed was the ancient religion of the Indians. He made his appearance in his pontifical

18

Fig. 4. — Mask from the Canadian Lenape. E. T. Tefft collection,
American Museum of Natural History. (Height of head, 14 in.)

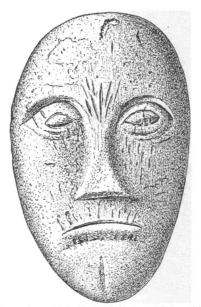

Fig. 5. — Stone head or Mĭsi'ngw' from Ohio. (Height, 13.9 in.)

garb, which was a coat of bear skins, dressed with the hair on, and hanging down to his toes; a pair of bear skin stockings; and a great wooden face painted, the one half black, the other half tawny, about the color of an Indian's skin, with an extravagant mouth, cut very much awry; the face fastened to a bear skin cap, which was drawn over his head. He advanced toward me with the instrument in his hand, which he used for music, in his idolatrous worship, which was a dry tortoise shell with some corn in it, and the neck of it drawn on to a piece of wood, which made a very convenient handle. As he came forward, he beat his tune with the rattle, and danced with all his might, but he did not suffer any part of his body, not so much as his fingers, to be seen."

With the exception of one minor point, the "wry mouth," this would be a good description of the Misĭ'ngwʻ outfit used until recently by the Lenape in Oklahoma (pi. 11). On the following page, Brainerd mentions "images" which seem to be the Mĭsi'ngwʻ faces carved on the posts of the Big House.

Zeisberger [29] also refers to the masks in these words:

"The only idol which the Indians have, and which may properly be called an idol, is their *Wsinkhoalican,* that is image. It is an image cut in wood, representing a human head in miniature, which they always carry about them either on a string around their neck or in a bag. They often bring offerings to it. In their houses of sacrifice they have a head of this idol as large as life put upon a pole in the middle of the room."

In his Dictionary, Zeisberger gives the word for "idol" as *mĕ'sink',* so it seems probable that the *W* in "Wsinkhoalikan" is a misprint for *M.*

MOTHER CORN

One of the important *manĭ'towŭk* of the old days was the Corn Goddess, known as "Mother Corn" of whom one of the Unami legends collected by the writer relates that "It was God's will that the Corn Spirit abide in the far heavenly region in the image of an aged woman, with dominion over all vegetation." Although little remembrance of the details of her worship can now be found among the Oklahoma Lenape, she is mentioned as a Guardian Spirit; while at the Minsi ceremonies at Grand River Reserve in Ontario, she was one of the twelve benefactors of mankind to whom the thanks of the people were offered, and Minsi women mentioned "Sister Corn" in praying for good crops in the corn fields; while Zeisberger [30] says that the presiding *Manĭ'to* of Indian Corn or maize was spoken of as the "wife" of the Indian, and was offered bear's flesh.

20

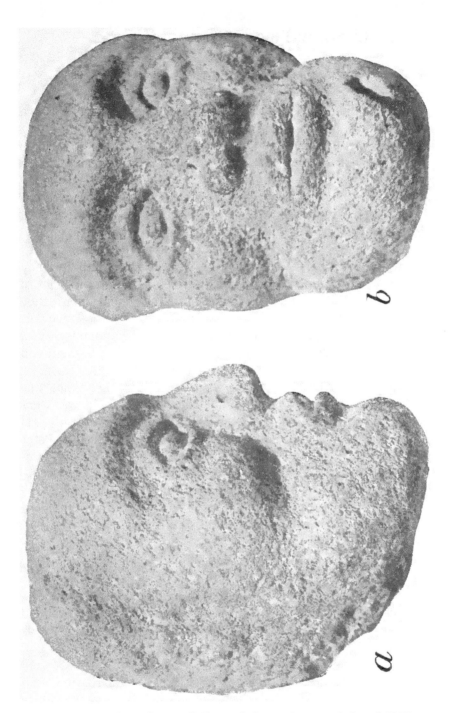

Stone head or Mĭsi'ngw', from Staten Island N.Y.

(Staten Island Institute of Arts and Sciences) (Plate IV.)

Chapter Two - Minor Deities

Doll Being

The masks described in the last chapter are merely representations of a supernatural being, and are not supposed to be the dwellings of a spirit or spirits except when worn by an impersonator, who is said to become imbued with the spirit when the mask is donned; nor are they usually supposed to possess inherent power, except as symbols of Mǐsinghâ-li'kŭn. But the Lenape had also a class of images, usually of wood, representing the human form, which were supposed to possess life, or at least to be the residence of spirits, which, so far as can be learned, had no separate existence. They were supposed to understand what was said to them, and to have the power of protecting the owner's health, to enjoy offerings, resent ill-treatment, and in fact seem to fall into the class of true fetishes. Usually, but not always, representing the female figure, they were kept as a rule by women, and were given yearly feasts, at which outfits of new clothes were put on them. The native name in Unami is *O" das;* in Minsi, *Nani'tis.* The ceremonies and beliefs associated with them will be described later, in the chapter on minor ceremonies. Most of the early writers seem to have overlooked them, which is not surprising, since they were matters of personal and not of public concern, and their rites were held in private. John Brainerd, however, mentions an "idol image" [31] which seems to be of this class, and a Minsi specimen is figured by Peter Jones [32] and mentioned by him in a footnote. This was afterward procured by the writer from Jones' son, and is now in the American Museum of Natural History (pi. vin). John Brainerd (brother of the better known David) made his note of the custom about the middle of the eighteenth century, while that of Jones dates from about a century later.

Tornado

Besides the gods hitherto named there were many other deities of lesser importance. The tornado, for instance, was one of these beings classed as *manǐ'towŭk.* He is mentioned as a giant in size, walking on his hands when in action, his long hair entangling and sweeping away forests and villages; and sometimes as a winged being. When a "cyclone" was seen approaching, some would burn tobacco, and addressing the roaring monster, as "Grandfather," would pray that he turn aside and leave the village in peace. Others, scorning such measures of conciliation, would burn old moccasins and rubbish, advising the destroyer to turn aside if he wished to escape the stinging smoke; while still others, even less conciliatory, threatened him with the edge of an axe, vowing they would "break a wing for him" if he came their way. It was commonly said in the tribe that on account of these practices the Lenape suffered little from this evil *manĭ'to*.

Snow Boy

Another minor *manĭ'to* is Snow Boy, a being who is supposed to control snow and ice, but who is different from "Our Grandfather at the North," who merely supplies the north wind. Offerings were made to Snow Boy to insure a proper amount of snow for tracking in the winter hunt. Further information concerning these last two *manĭ'towŭk* will be found in the paper on Lenape Mythology, now in preparation.

Comet

There is a third *manĭ'to* called *Elau'nato*, which some Lenape say means "Comet," others "Shooting Star." When a war is impending, says the legend, this being may be seen flying through the air, carrying a bunch of human heads. After Elau'nato has passed, if one listens he will hear a distant rumbling sound, for this *manĭ'to* knows beforehand where the fighting will take place, and drops the heads on the spot, and the noise of their fall is a roar like thunder.

Evil Manĭ'towuk

Both the Great Horned Serpents, monsters living in the rivers and lakes, and the Giant Bear were considered evil *manĭ'towŭk*, the only good derived from them being, in the first case, charms made of the scales, bone, or horn of the monsters, supposed to bring rain; and, in the second case, a medicine made from the tooth said to have the power of healing wounds. Children were accustomed to hunt in the sand for tracks of the Little People, comparable with fairies or elves among the whites.

Animal Spirits

The concepts regarding the numerous animal spirits who were believed to offer themselves as guardians for mankind, are rather hard to define. Most Indians seem to regard their mysterious animal helper not as the spirit or soul of any particular animal taken as an individual, but as a spirit representing the entire species as a whole and partaking of the nature of the species, at the same time having human and *manĭ'to* attributes.

Brainerd [33] makes some interesting remarks on this subject, which are worth quoting:

"They do not indeed suppose a divine power *essential* to, or *inhering* in, these creatures; but that some invisible beings...communicate to these animals a *great power; ...*and so make these creatures the immediate authors of good to certain persons. Whence such a creature becomes sacred to the persons to whom he is supposed to be the immediate author of good, and through him they must worship the invisible powers, though to others he is no more than any other creature."

Certain it is, if a Lenape states that his blessing or power comes from "the otter," he does not mean some particular otter, but a spirit otter whose existence is independent of the life of any particular animal. However, such an animal was supposed, like a man, to have a spirit or soul of its own.

Plant Spirits

When gathering herbs for medicine it was customary to offer prayers to certain spirits. Some seem to have prayed at this time to the four directions, others to the presiding genius of the species of plants they sought, or to the spirit of the individual plant itself. The Minsi say that only certain plants were thus addressed. The Corn Spirit has already been mentioned.

Local Genii

Certain localities, it is said, were thought to be the dwellings of local genii, to whom offerings were occasionally made, especially such places as displayed curious or unusual natural features, while even certain stones were said to have an animate principle or indwelling spirit.

Chapter Three - Survival of the Soul

The Soul

The doctrine of the survival of the soul or spirit after the death of the body, forms an integral part of Lenape belief. The spirit is supposed to leave the body at the moment of dissolution, but remains in the vicinity eleven days, during which time it subsists on food found in the houses of the living, if none has been placed at the grave. Some say that the actual food is not consumed but that the ghost extracts some essence or nourishment from it.

The Land of Spirits

On the twelfth day the spirit leaves the earth and makes its way to the twelfth or highest heaven, the home of the Creator, where it lives indefinitely in a veritable "Happy Hunting Ground," a beautiful country where life goes on much as it does on earth, except that pain, sickness, and sorrow are unknown, and distasteful work and worry have no place; where children shall meet their parents who have gone before, and parents their children; where everything always looks new and bright. There is no sun in the Land of Spirits, but a brighter light which the Creator has provided. All people who die here, be they young or old, will look the same age there, and the blind, cripples, — anyone who has been maimed or injured, — will be perfect and as good as any there. This is because the flesh only was injured, not the spirit.

This paradise, however, is only for the good, for those who have been kind to their fellows and have done their duty by their people. Little is said of those who have done evil in this world, except that they are excluded from the happy Land of Spirits. Some Unami say that the blood in a dead body draws up into globular form and floats about in the air as a luminous ball, but this is not the true spirit.

The Minsi seem to have retained a more archaic belief, for they say that the Land of Spirits lies to the southwest, in a country of good hunting. Here they say, the wigwams of the spirits are always neat and clean, and happiness prevails. But between our world and the spirit country flows a river which the spirit must cross on a slender foot-log or in a canoe.

Ghosts and Mediumship

Ghosts do not seem always to have left the earth at the expiration of the twelve days, or else they have the power of returning, for the Lenape claim that boys, dreaming for power, have sometimes been pitied and given some blessing by the ghosts, who remained their guardian spirits through life. Such people were considered to have the power of talking with the departed and sometimes made a practice of it, but mediumship was by no means confined to them. Among the Minsi formerly they were accustomed to hold meetings in the burial grounds at certain times, when some medium, it is said, would communicate with the spirits.

The late James Wolf, one of the principal Minsi informants, was said to have this power. One time a man was drowned in the Thames river near Munceytown in Ontario, and the body could not be located. Wolf, it is said, walked up and down the river-banks, with a companion, talking to the water. At last a strange sound was heard, and Wolf stopped. "That was the dead man's spirit," he said; "the body lies right over in that hole."

Surely enough, when they procured a boat, they found the body in the hole, wedged beneath a sunken log.

Certain regular ceremonies were held by both the Unami and the Minsi in honor of the dead, and will be discussed in a later paper.

Early Accounts

Penn. — In William Penn's letter, [34] dated August 16, 1683, is the first mention of any details of Lenape beliefs regarding the soul that has been found. He says:

"They say there is a King that made them, who dwells in a glorious Country to the Southward of them, and that the Souls of the Good shall go thither, where they shall live again."

Brainerd. — The same Indian whom Brainerd saw in 1745 dressed in a bearskin costume and with a wooden mask, told him [35] that —

"departed souls all went southward, and that the difference between good and bad was this: that the former were admitted into a beautiful town with spiritual walls, and that the latter would forever hover around these walls, in vain attempts to get in."

Later, [36] Brainerd speaks of the Spirit Land of the Lenape to the southward as being "an unknown and curious place" in which the shadows of the dead "will enjoy some kind of happiness, such as hunting, feasting, dancing, and the like."

One of his Indian informants defined the kind of "bad folks" who would be unhappy in the hereafter as "those who lie, steal, quarrel with their neighbors, are unkind to their friends, and especially to aged parents, and, in a word, such as are a plague to mankind." These would be excluded from the "Happy Hunting Ground," not so much as a punishment to themselves, as to keep them from rendering unhappy the spirits of the good inhabiting the "beautiful town."

Zeisberger. — About 1748, according to Zeisberger, [37] a number of preachers appeared among the Indians, who claimed to have traveled in Heaven and conversed with God. Some exhibited charts of deerskin upon which were drawn maps of the Land of Spirits and figures representing other subjects used in their preaching. Some of their ideas concerning the Son of God, the Devil, and Hell, are evidently derived from the whites; others seem more aboriginal in character, such as purification by emetics, twelve different kinds being used. He wrote:

"Other teachers pretended that stripes were the most effectual means to purge away sin. They advised their hearers to suffer themselves to be beaten with twelve different sticks from the soles of their feet to their necks, that their sins might pass from them through their throats. They preached a system of morals, very severe for the savages, insisting that the Indians abstain from fornication, adultery, murder, theft, and practise virtuous living as the condition to their attaining after death the place of good spirits, which they call Tschipeghacki, the 'land of spirits,' where the life is happy, and deer, bear and all manner of game are abundant and the water is like crystal. There nought was to be heard save singing, dancing and merry making...The passage thither is the Milky Way...

Whoever reaches that place will find a city of beautiful houses and clean streets. Entering a house he will see no one, but have good things to eat placed before him, a fire made and a bed prepared — all of which is done by spirits invisible to him. Others assert that such an one will see the women coming with baskets on their backs full of strawberries and bilberries, large as apples, and will observe the inhabitants daily appear in fine raiment and live a life of rejoicing. — The bad Indians ...will not reach the place, Tschipeghacki, but must remain some distance away, able to see those within dwelling happily, but not able to enter. They would receive nothing but poisonous wood and poisonous roots to eat, holding them ever near the brink of a bitter death, but not suffering them to die."

Zeisberger usually specifies when his information is derived from tribes other than the Lenape, from whom most of his data were procured; so it is probable that the following quotation applies to them, although in part somewhat at variance with our other knowledge. He says: [38]

"They believe in the immortality of the soul. Some liken themselves to corn which, when thrown out and buried in the soil, comes up and grows. Some believe their souls to be in the sun, and only their bodies here. Others say that when they die their souls will go to God, and suppose that when they have been some time with God they will be at liberty to return to the world and be born again. Hence many believe...that they may have been in the world before.

"They believe also in the transmigration of the soul. Wandering spirits and ghosts, they claim, sometimes throw something into a public path and whoever goes over it is bewitched and becomes lame or ill."

Such was the Lenape belief with regard to the powers that control the world, and such were his notions concerning the souls of men. The main channel of communication between this great supernatural realm and mankind was, to the Lenape as to so many other tribes of Indians, the dream or vision, experienced either while fasting or in natural sleep. This subject will be considered in the next chapter.

Chapter Four - Visions and Guardian Spirits

The most vital and intimate phase of Lenape religion is the belief in dreams and visions, and in the existence of personal guardian spirits or supernatural helpers — concepts of wide distribution among the North American tribes, but rarely, perhaps, so vivid or well-developed as we find them here. The vision was the point of contact, the channel of communication, in Lenape belief, between the great and marvelous supernatural world and the sphere of everyday human life. In a vision the youth first found his guardian spirit, to whom he would always appeal, as his own special friend in the supernatural hierarchy, for aid and comfort in time of trouble, and for the revelation of coming events. He felt that this being took a close personal interest in his affairs, while the greater gods, including the Great Spirit himself, were so remote and so occupied with controlling more important things that they might not notice or concern themselves with the affairs of one individual man. Therefore the bulk of his prayers and offerings went to his guardian spirit. If a Lenape won great success on a war expedition or a hunting trip, he was sure the spirit had helped him; if unlucky, he believed that for some reason his guardian had become estranged, or had been overpowered by superior and malevolent forces. A man might become a sorcerer or a shaman at the behest of his guardian spirit, given in a dream or vision, or change his mode of life in other ways. Not every Lenape was blessed with such a guardian; yet many were so favored, usually in their boyhood days. To be eligible for supernatural favor, the youth had to *pi'lsŭn,* or pure, which means that not only must he be chaste, but that he must have kept strictly all the taboos against eating food prepared by women in their periodic condition, etc. Old Lenape say that, as the children of the tribe are reared nowadays in the same way as the whites, they can no longer be *pi'lsŭn,* and the Powers will speak to them no more. This is a sad matter, for it means the loss of their principal ancient ceremonies, at which only those blessed with a vision can take active part. The old people feel it keenly that there will be no one left to conduct the rites when the last of their generation has been laid away.

Initiation of Boys

Parents were especially anxious, of course, that their sons should have supernatural aid, hence, when a boy reached the age of about twelve years, they would frequently pretend to abuse him, and would drive him, fasting, out into the forest to shift as best he might, in the hope that some *manǐ'to* would take pity on the suffering child and grant him some power or blessing that would be his dependence through life.

Sometimes a man who had several sons would take them out into the forest and build them a rude little tent, and here they would remain for days at a time. During the day the boys were not permitted to eat, but just before sunrise every morning each was given a medicine to make him vomit, after which a tiny piece of meat was given him, about the size of a man's little finger. Occasionally the boys became able to fast in this way for twelve days, at the end of which time, the Lenape say, some had received such power that they were able to rise into the air, or go down into the ground, or prophesy events a year or two ahead, with the magic aid of the supernatural being that had taken pity on them.

Other Visions

It sometimes happened also that people received visions of power in natural sleep without fasting, or even when wide awake, while feeling melancholy and heartsick over the death of a loved one, or suffering other misfortune or trouble.

As they sat brooding, some *manï'to* might address himself to them, and give them advice and comfort, or endow them with some kind of power. Women occasionally had visions of this kind.

The Guardian Spirit

Whatever the precise circumstances of its appearance, the guardian spirit in many instances was said to show itself first in human form, and it was only when it turned to leave that its real shape (of an animal, for instance) was noticed by the recipient of its blessing. Sometimes the interview was quite long and the directions given by the *manï'to* (for ceremonies, etc.) quite explicit; on other occasions they were very vague and cryptic. Frequently, according to the stories told, some tangible object, called by the Unami the *opi'na,* or blessing, was handed by the *manï'to* to the recipient of his favor, who usually swallowed it. Some recipients were called on, however, to make and keep some symbol of their protector, ^ which was usually worn on the person in the form of a charm.

Favored Individuals. — Persons favored with a guardian spirit usually became prominent among their people and were held in high esteem. They composed rythmic chants referring to their visions for use at the Annual Ceremony (which will be discussed in the next chapter), and dance songs to accompany them. Rarely were the words of either chants or songs at all definite: as a rule they merely mentioned attributes of the singer's guardian, or incidents of their first meeting, without stating outright what the guardian spirit was, or telling a consecutive story of the vision.

Most Lenape who have had such visions can not be induced to tell the details; but the following examples of such experiences, imperfect in many points, were finally obtained. Incomplete though they are, they will give some idea of this class of beliefs and in this way may prove of value.

Unami Examples. — One old man named Pokite'hemun ("Breaker"), known to the whites in Oklahoma as George Wilson, saw in his vision what seemed to be a man who held out to him a white round object like a boy's marble, then tossed it to him. Pokite'hemun caught it and swallowed it. Then as it turned to go, the being cried "*Kwank! kwank! kwank! The ducks have a praying meeting in the fall of the year!*" As it turned, Pokite'hemun noticed that it was really a duck instead of a man, and was colored half black and half white. [39]

Pokite'hemun could pound on his chest at any time and apparently cough up a round marble-like object, which he would show in his hand and then appear to swallow again. This he claimed was the opi'na given by his guardian spirit.

He seemed to regard the words of the duck spirit as an admonition to do all he could to keep up the tribal Annual Ceremony, which was held in the fall; while the "blessing" gave him good fortune. The chant he composed for use at this ceremony is as follows:

> *Lawulĕnjei*
> *Wŭnjegŭk toxweyu*
> *Kwĕnnanowagŭn*
> *Wailangomanole*
> *Lĕnape, eli nanŭn*
> *Telowan, Iowan*
> *Nunni, ĕndageko*
> *Lowaet, Iowa nŭnni.*

The interpreter's translation, which is a somewhat free one, follows:

> "When he opened his hand
> Something came out of the center
> That's his blessing
> (For?) our kinfolks, the
>
> Lenape; because that
> Is what he said, he did say
> This, when
> He spoke, he said this."

Then came the dance song:

30

He-e-e-e nehani
Latamaɴne
Nehani lamaɴne
Kweɴnanowagŭn, nowagŭn
Hayelaɴgomaɴ
Gweheyeha
Gehe!

This, according to the interpreter, means simply, when stripped of its superfluous syllables, "We own a temple — his blessing — our kinfolks."

Another man saw in his boyhood vision the Misinghâli'kŭn, or Living Solid Face, riding on a deer. I was unable to get the details of their meeting, or the chant, but this is the dance song:

Hehotawege'na
Hotowege'na
Xingâlo' pai awhe'wani
Misinghâli'kŭn
Hâli'kŭne
A-he'-he-he'!

This, the interpreter said, means "Riding it, riding it, big buck deer, this one, Misinghâli'kŭn!" Seldom do the songs or chants refer so definitely to the protector as does this.

A third Lenape, when a boy, was sent out to the corn-field to drive away the crows. As he stood by the field he saw them flying around to light on a tree near by. Suddenly someone spoke to him, and among the things said (which were not revealed to me) were the words "I like this Lenape food," referring to the corn. The boy thought a man was addressing him, until the person suddenly flew away in the form of a crow, crying *"Ha! Ha! Ha!"* I failed to get the Indian words for the song, and my informant did not remember the chant, but the translation of the song was given as follows:

"I like this Lenape food:"
I never knew a crow said that
Till the crow was cawing
"Ha! Ha! Ha!"

A fourth had seen some kind of an animal in his vision, but never told any of his tribesmen what it was. His song, as now remembered, was translated thus:

Come, follow me,
I am going
Out into the country.

31

A fifth had "Mother Corn" (the Corn Spirit) for a guardian, but only part of his song is remembered.

> "All my children
> Are glad when I come out!"

Some people were helped by the spirits of the dead in the same way that others received aid from animal or other nature spirits.

"Old man" Secondine, now dead, a well-known Oklahoma Lenape, was one of these. When a boy his parents drove him out in the woods, as was the custom, in the hope that he might receive a supernatural helper. After wandering about for a time, he took refuge in a large hollow tree, and made that his camping place. Before long he was visited by apparitions of persons he knew to be dead, who took pity on his starving condition, and brought him food which they had taken at night from the houses of the living, this being the way that disembodied spirits are supposed to get nourishment when visiting the scenes of their earthly life. In the meantime his parents were unable to find him, and searched for him without avail until the ghosts finally revealed to them his camping place, and then he was brought safely home. Ever afterward he claimed the ghosts as his guardians, and like others blessed with this kind of helpers, was said to hold some kind of communication with the departed.

Minsi Examples. — The late James Wolf, my principal Minsi informant, was said to possess this power, as was stated in the preceding chapter. He had, moreover, received another vision when a boy, but had made little, if any, use of it, because of his profession of Christianity. One time in his boyhood days, he told me, he thought or dreamed (he was not asleep at the time) that there was no water in the river, and that he went down into its bed and found only one little hole containing water. In this was a creature resembling a catfish, yet somewhat different, and near it was an ordinary crayfish, while on the surface of the water walked a number of little flies. The boy thinking what he had seen was real, ran home in haste to tell his father. The father walked down with him to see, but stopped on the bank where the edge of the water had been, while the boy ran on down to his pool. The river-bed seemed dry to him, but his father would not come, saying that the river was full of water. The boy then came out and they started for home, but before they were out of sight, the lad looked back. To his surprise, the river was full as usual.

The father, who was Flying Wolf, a noted Minsi warrior, had been favored himself, when a boy, with a rather unusual sort of vision, which James Wolf related to me, as nearly as possible the way the old man used to tell it at the Annual Ceremony.

"When I was a boy, I was once fast asleep on a hill near a little creek. Someone said, 'Wake up! Let us go where our friends are!' So I got up and followed him across the little creek and up a hill, where I saw six men sitting on a log. Then I went up and shook hands with them all. After they had shaken hands with me they all danced around in a ring." At this point he used to sing one verse of his dance song —

Wĕmi wangontowak kewiha
All greet one another
Yoki lĕnape witci.
Now Lenape at the same time
E-ye-he-ye-ĕ!

"They told me, 'We will go to see our friends,' so I went with them. Every now and then they stopped and danced around as they had done before. After a while one of them told me to look toward the south, and there I saw a black cloud in which the lightning flashed. 'Would you like to go there?' they asked me. I answered 'No.' Then one asked if I wanted to go *that* way, pointing to the northeast, where the sky was blue and bright, to which I answered that I would rather go in that direction toward the clear sky. A little farther on they said: 'We will now leave you. Watch us as we go.' They went to the east a little way, and then I saw them trotting. They were wolves, and I had thought all the while that they were human beings."

Verses of the dance song were sung at intervals during this speech. From analogy with other visions, such as are recorded above, one would think that the six wolf-men must have become Flying Wolf's protectors, but instead, it was a Thunder Being that became his principal guardian, whose participation in the vision is merely inferred from the mention in the speech of the black cloud and the lightning. Evidently this Thunder Being was not offended when Flying Wolf told his guides that he would rather go toward the clear sky than toward the black cloud.

The Minsi say that when Flying Wolf recited his vision in the Big House ceremonies, he moved everyone, some even to tears. After he had finished, they say, a thunder-shower would almost always rise. He would become strangely excited when the dark clouds began to bank up on the horizon and spread themselves over the land. Stripping himself to the breechcloth, he was ready to go out when the storm broke, for he would never stay beneath a roof at such a time. He loved to expose his body to the driving gusts of wind and rain; the appalling roar was music to his ears; while the lighting, to the eyes of the frightened onlookers, seemed to play about his very body. He used to say that if he stayed indoors the lightning display would be so terrible that the others in the house could not endure it. No wonder they used to say of him, *"Piles' waL pewa'latcil!"* "He is in league with the Thunders!", or better, perhaps, "The Thunders will protect him!"

Within the memory of Minsi now living in Canada there were two members of the tribe who claimed the Sun spirit, *Ki'zho* (or *Ki'zhox*) as their protector. One of these was known as "Old man" Halfmoon, the other as "Muncey John" Henry. Halfmoon, it is said, when he wished to appear as a warrior, would sometimes hold his bare hands up toward the flaming face of his guardian, then rub the palms down his cheeks. When he removed his hands, it was seen that his face, clean before, was now painted in brilliant colors! "Surely," the people cried, "this man is in league with the Sun!"

That the idea of a tangible 'blessing' is found among the Minsi, as well as among the Unami, is shown in certain of their traditions.

Historical References. — *Brainerd.* — Brainerd seems to have been about the first author to recognize in any degree the importance of the dream or vision in Lenape religious belief. He says: [40]

"They give much heed to *dreams,* because they suppose that these invisible powers give them directions at such times about certain affairs, and sometimes inform them what *animal* they would choose to be worshipped in."

Other remarks by Brainerd on the same general topic were quoted in the preceding chapter.

Zeisberger. — Zeisberger [41] also devotes a paragraph to it, in which he says:

"Almost all animals and the elements are looked upon as spirits, one exceeding the other in dignity and power. There is scarcely an Indian who does not believe that one or more of these spirits has not been particularly given him to assist him and make him prosper. This, they claim, has been made known to them in a dream, even as their religious belief and witchcraft has been made known to them in a dream. One has, in a dream, received a serpent or a buffalo, another the sun or the moon, another an owl or some other bird, another a fish, some even ridiculously insignificant creatures such as ants. These are considered their spirits or *Manittos.* If an Indian has no Manitto to be his friend he considers himself forsaken, has nothing on which he may lean, has no hope of any assistance and is small in his own eyes. On the other hand those who have been thus favored possess a high and proud spirit."

Loskiel. — Loskiel's account [42] seems largely derived from the above. He remarks:

"The *manittos* are also considered as tutelar spirits. Every Indian has one or more, which he conceives to be peculiarly given to assist him and make him prosper. One has in a dream received the sun as his tutelar spirit, another the moon; a third, an owl; a fourth, a buff aloe; and so forth. An Indian is dispirited, and considers himself as forsaken by God, till he has received a tutelar spirit in a dream; But those who have been thus favored, are full of courage, and proud of their powerful ally."

Heckewelder. — Heckewelder [43] devotes a whole chapter to the subject, under the head of "Initiation of Boys," to which the reader is referred, as it is all of interest, but can not be reproduced here. I will merely quote portions of one paragraph, which will serve to show that this author found approximately similar ideas as had his predecessors, concepts which still exist among the Lenape.

"When a boy is to be thus *initiated,* he is put under an alternate course of physic and fasting...so that he sees, or fancies that he sees visions, and has extraordinary dreams. Then he has interviews with the Manitto or with spirits, who inform him of what he was before he was born, and what he will be after his death. His fate in this life is laid entirely open before him, the spirit tells him what is to be his future employment, whether he will be a valiant warrior, a mighty hunter, a doctor, a conjuror or a prophet."

Later in the chapter Heckewelder mentions the fact that persons favored with such dreams considered themselves under the protection of the "celestial powers," and mentions the "strength, the power, and the courage" conveyed to them, but lays more stress on the prophetic side of these visions than on the actual aid rendered, according to Lenape belief, by the supernatural guardians.

Adams. — From Heckewelder's time to the present, I know of but one writer, besides myself, who describes, from his own observation, the Lenape belief in visions and guardian spirits. This is R. C. Adams, [44] himself of Delaware blood, whose notes may be found in the volume on Indians of the United States Census Report for 1890 (p. 298 et seq.). He says:

"It is believed by the Delawares that every one has a guardian spirit which comes in the form of some bird, animal, or other thing, at times in dreams, and tells them what to do and what will happen. The guardian spirit is sent from the Great Spirit."

Having now considered the very foundation of Lenape religion, we may turn with better understanding, to their great Annual Ceremony.

Lenape Ceremonial House near Dewey, Oklahoma (Plate V.)

Chapter Five - Unami Annual Ceremony

The Leader

The great Annual Ceremony of the Lenape now in Oklahoma was and is held when the leaves turn yellow in the fall of the year, usually, according to the "pale face" reckoning, some time between the tenth and twentieth of October. It is not exactly a tribal affair, although the whole tribe participates, but must be undertaken by some certain individual of the proper qualifications who takes the responsibility of "bringing in" the meeting and acting as a leader.

The phratry to which this leader belongs determines the exact form of the ceremonies to be held; for each totemic group has a ritual of its own, that of the Wolf, which is here related, differing in some particulars from the ceremonies as practised by the Turtle or Turkey people. In former times, it is said, when one phratry had finished its twelve days of ceremonies, another would enact theirs, followed by the third; but at present qualified leaders are so few that it seldom if ever happens that more than one of them feels able to accept such exacting duties in any one year.

This leader it is who sends a messenger forth to notify the people what day the ceremonies are to commence and to invite them all to attend.

Several days before the date the wagons begin to roll in and a white village of tents springs up about the gray walls of the old Big House, temple, or *xi'ngwikan* (pl. v), standing on the banks of Little Caney river, north of Dewey in northern Oklahoma, far from any human habitation.

Built of rough logs, the Big House is now provided with a roof of hand-split shingles pierced by two great smoke-holes, as shown in the frontispiece and in pl. V, VI, but in former days the roof was of bark. The length is about 40 ft. from east to west, with a height at the eaves of about 6 ft., at the ridge 14 ft., and a width of 24.5 ft. Aside from certain ingenuities of construction which can not be discussed here, its chief interest lies in the two large carvings of the human face, one facing east (fig. 6) and one west, which adorn the great central post supporting the ridgepole. Similar carvings, but smaller, may be seen upon each of the six posts which support the logs forming the sides (fig. 7), and still smaller ones, one upon each of the four door-posts. All twelve faces are painted, the right side of each red, the left black. The building is used only for the Annual Ceremony.

Fig. 6.— Central post of Ceremonial House, showing carved face.

Fig. 7. — Side posts of Ceremonial House, showing carved faces.

Officers

The messenger sent to assemble the people is one of three male attendants chosen by the leader, and these three men appoint three women to serve also. To these six attendants, known as *a'ckas,* falls all the laborious work of the meeting. Although the duties are menial, it is considered quite an honor to be selected as *a'ckas.* The attendants camp on the north and south sides of the little open square just east of the Big House (pi. vn), an area where no one is allowed to pitch a tent.

Other officers selected for the meeting are a speaker (usually at the time of the writer's visit, Chief Charley Elkhair), two singers, called *Tale'gunŭk,* "Cranes," whose duty it is to beat the dry deerskin drum and sing the necessary songs, and a chief hunter who is supposed to provide venison for the feast.

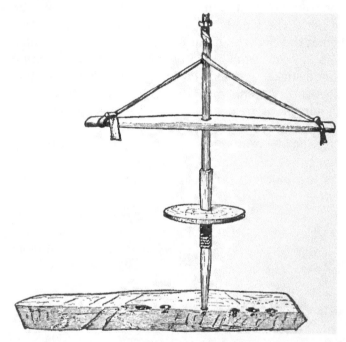

Fig. 8. — Ceremonial fire-drill used at the Annual Ceremony. (Length of shaft, 29.5 in.)

Preparations

Arrived at the Big House, the attendants begin at once to prepare the building for use after its year of idleness. The first act of the men is to make mortar of mud, in the old style, and stop the cracks between the logs of the house. Then they cut two forked saplings, and set them in the ground about ten feet apart, some distance in front of the Big House (see pi. vn); upon these is laid a pole, running east and west, to support the twenty-gallon kettle used in preparing hominy for the feast. After this they gather about a cord of wood for the fires inside the Big House and the cooking fire outside. Then the first night, a fire pure and undefined by the white man and his matches, is made with a fire-drill (fig. 8). This is operated on the principal of a pump-drill, like the ceremonial fire-drills of the Iroquois. This fire, and this only, may be used in the temple, and no one is permitted to take it outside for any purpose.

38

Lenape Annual Ceremony in Progress

Native Painting by Earnest Spybuck, a Shawnee (Plate VI.)

Ceremony Commenced

Two of the attendants, a man and a woman, then build the two fires in the temple, so that there may be plenty of light, and sweep the floor with turkey-wings for brushes. The men attendants take turns so that one of them, at least, is always on guard outside the building. When the temple is clean, the fires are burning bright, and the *a'ckas* have called the people in and all are assembled, the chief arises and delivers a speech.

Chief's Speech

First he states the rules of the meeting, then he speaks along some such line as the following, which was dictated by Chief Elkhair, who frequently made these speeches:

"We are thankful that so many of us are alive to meet together here once more, and that we are ready to hold our ceremonies in good faith. Now we shall meet here twelve nights in succession to pray to Gicelĕmû"kaong, who has directed us to worship in this way. And these twelve Mĭsi'ngw‘ faces [carved on the posts of the house] are here to watch and to carry our prayers to Gicelĕmû"kaong in the highest heaven. The reason why we dance at this time is to raise our prayers to him. Our attendants here, three women and three men, have the task of keeping everything about our Temple in good order, and of trying to keep peace, if there is trouble. They must haul wood and build fires, cook and sweep out the Big House.

"When they sweep, they must sweep both sides of the fire twelve times, which sweeps a road to Heaven, just as they say that it takes twelve years to reach it. Women in their menses must not enter this house.

"When we come into this house of ours we are glad, and thankful that we are well, and for everything that makes us feel good which the Creator has placed here for our use. We come here to pray Him to have mercy on us for the year to come and to give us everything to make us happy; may we have good crops, and no dangerous storms, floods nor earthquakes. We all realize what He has put before us all through life, and that He has given us a way to pray to Him and thank Him. We are thankful to the East because everyone feels good in the morning when they awake, and see the bright light coming from the East, and when the Sun goes down in the West we feel good and glad we are well; then we are thankful to the West. And we are thankful to the North, because when the cold winds come we are glad to have lived to see the leaves fall again; and to the South, for when the south wind blows and everything is coming up in the spring, we are glad to live to see the grass growing and everything green again. We thank the Thunders, for they are the *manĭ'towŭk* that bring the rain,

41

which the Creator has given them power to rule over. And we thank our mother, the Earth, whom we claim as mother because the Earth carries us and everything we need. When we eat and drink and look around, we know it is Gicelĕmû"kaong that makes us feel good that way. He gives us the purest thoughts that can be had. We should pray to Him every morning.

"Man has a spirit, and the body seems to be a coat for that spirit. That is why people should take care of their spirits, so as to reach Heaven and be admitted to the Creator's dwelling. We are given some length of time to live on earth, and then our spirits must go. When anyone's time comes to leave this earth, he should go to Gicelĕmû"kaong, feeling good on the way. We all ought to pray to Him, to prepare ourselves for days to come so that we can be with Him after leaving the earth.

"We must all put our thoughts to this meeting, so that Gicelĕmû"kaong will look upon us and grant what we ask. You all come here to pray; you have a way to reach Him all through life. Do not think of evil; strive always to think of the good which He has given us.

"When we reach that place, we shall not have to do anything or worry about anything, only live a happy life. We know there are many of our fathers who have left this earth and are now in this happy place in the Land of Spirits. When we arrive we shall see our fathers, mothers, children, and sisters there. And when we have prepared ourselves so that we can go to where our parents and children are, we feel happy.

"Everything looks more beautiful there than here, everything looks new, and the waters and fruits and everything are lovely.

"No sun shines there, but a light much brighter than the sun, the Creator makes it brighter by his power. All people who die here, young or old, will be of the same age there; and those who are injured, crippled, or made blind will look as good as the rest of them. It is nothing but the flesh that is injured: the spirit is as good as ever. That is the reason that people are told to help always the cripples or the blind. Whatever you do for them will surely bring its reward. Whatever you do for anybody will bring you credit hereafter. Whenever we think the thoughts that Gicelĕmû"kaong has given us, it will do us good.

"This is all I can think of to say along this line. Now we will pass the Turtle around, and all that feel like worshiping maytakeit and perform their ceremonies."

Some nights the speaker says more, sometimes less, just as he feels, but he always tries to tell it as he heard it from the old people who came before him.

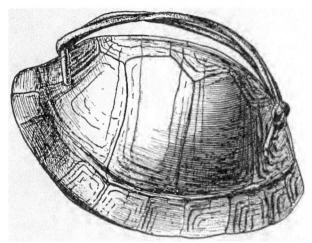

Fig. 9. — Rattle of land-tortoise shell, used by celebrants at the Annual Ceremony. (Length, 4.2 in.)

Recital of Visions

Now, as was stated, these meetings are "brought in" by individuals; that is a certain person, usually a man, undertakes to arrange for the meeting and to lead the ceremonies. This person must be one of those gifted by a vision or dream of power in their youth, and hence, according to Lenape belief, one in communication with the supernatural world.

When the people file into the Big House, the few that still have them dressed in their best Indian costumes carefully preserved for such occasions (pl. i), the members of this leader's clan always take their seats on the north side, the other two clans in the west end and the south side. Men and women, however, do not mingle, but sit separately in the space allotted to their common clan. The diagram (pi. vii) shows the seating of the clans when the ceremony is "brought in" by a member of the Wolf division.

After the chief's speech, the leader arises from his place just north of the central post, and, rapidly shaking a rattle (*taxo'xi cowŭni'gŭn*) made of a box-tortoise shell (fig. 9), recites his vision in a high monotone, word by word. After he utters each word, he pauses an instant to give the singers sitting at the rolled dry deerskin called

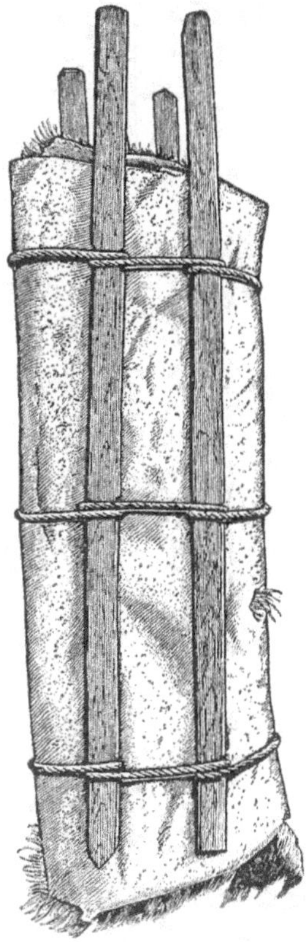

Fig. 10. — Drum made of dried deerskin used at the Annual Ceremony. (Length 38.2 in.)

43

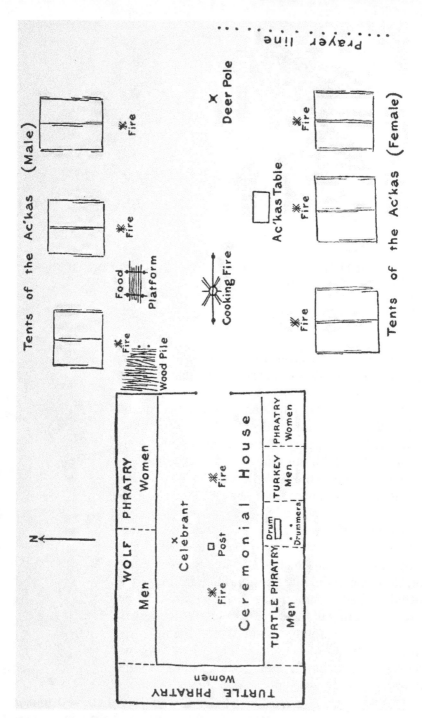

Plan of Lanape Ceremonial House and Grounds Near Dewey, Oklahoma
(Plate VII)

44

powŭni'gŭn which serves as a drum (fig. 10), ample time to repeat the same word in the same tone, which produces an extraordinary effect. When he finishes, the drummers beat rapidly on the dry hide, repeating *"Ho-o-o!"* a number of times.

Then the celebrant repeats a verse of his song in the same way, and the drummers, having learned the words, sing them to a dance tune, beating the drum in slower time. After dancing awhile, the celebrator whoops, and they stop; then another similar verse, if not the same, is recited and then sung,

When the leader dances, he circles about the two fires contra-clockwise, and those who wish may join in the dance and follow him (pl. vi).

His dance finished, the leader passes the turtle-shell to the next man who has been blessed with a vision. This one has the privilege of singing his vision if he wishes; if not, it is handed to the next "dreamer." After a celebrant has taken his seat, it is customary for those who desire it to smoke until the next man is ready to commence. At this time also it is considered proper for the people to enter or leave the Big House, which is not permitted while the actual ceremony is in progress. When the turtle rattle has thus made the round of the building and gets back to its starting point, the meeting is brought to a close. This is usually along toward morning, the exact time of course being dependent on the number who have sung their visions, and on the length of the intermissions.

Conclusion of Rites

Now, when the man who started the ceremonies begins to dance, that is a signal for two of the women *a'ckas,* or attendants, to go out and pound corn for hominy or meal, and two of their men colleagues cook it in the kettle hanging on the pole, so that it is ready when the turtle has made its rounds and the meeting is about to close. Then the repast of hominy or corn mush called *sä'pan* is distributed, and the speaker says, "We will now pray twelve times," so twelve times they cry *"Ho-o-o!"* as a prayer. Then they feast, using musselshells from the river as spoons, and finally the speaker dismisses them with the words, "This is all for tonight; tomorrow night we will meet again."

Departure of the Hunters

When the next night arrives, approximately the same performance is repeated; and the same the next, with little of interest occurring during the day; but on the fourth morning, the leader who has selected a man for chief hunter, gives him a yard of wampum as pay. This master of the hunt then selects as many assistants as he wants, and he and his crew all gather in the Big House, where they are served about noon with a feast prepared for the occasion by the women of the camp, and the attendants tie sacks of the food to the hunters' saddles.

When they have finished eating, they arrange themselves in a row, each hunter standing on his left foot and barely touching the ground with the toes of his right, an action whose meaning I have not yet been able to determine.

Then the speaker rises and talks to them, and the Mĭsi'ngwʻ who has been seen about the camp from time to time, is in the Big House listening to his words. "When you hunt," says the speaker, "think of nothing but luck to kill deer." As he speaks he goes to the west fire and throws into it, six times, an offering of native tobacco; then to the east fire, where he sacrifices six more pinches of the sacred herb — twelve in all. While sacrificing tobacco, he prays to the Mĭsi'ngwʻ to drive the deer up, so that the hunters can kill them. As he drops the last tobacco into the flames, he says, "If you kill a deer right away, bring it in tonight; if not, bring in all you kill day after tomorrow."

What tobacco is left is given to the chief hunter with the words, "When you camp tonight, burn this and ask Mĭsinghâli'kŭn to let you kill deer." The reader will remember that Mĭsinghâli'kŭn, in whose image the Mĭsi'ngwʻ is carved, is supposed to have control over the deer, and in fact over all wild animals.

All the hunters that are in the habit of chewing tobacco are now given some for this purpose. When they file out and mount their horses, the Mĭsi'ngwʻ follows them and sees them off.

After the hunters have disappeared, the people call the Mĭsi'ngwʻ back into the Big House and coax him to dance, while two men volunteer to sing for him.

Prayer for the Hunters

The following evening six men are appointed and given a yard of wampum to divide among them, to go out close to the forked game-pole east of the Big House, intended for the carcasses of the deer, and "pray" there twelve times. The meaning of this, of course, is that they sound the prayer word *"Ho-o-o!"* which is evidently to help the hunters. This night also a yard of wampum is unstrung and scattered on the ground just west of the east fire, and this the attendants must pick up, crying *"Ho-o-o!"* as they do so. For doing this, which is called "picking berries," they are supposed to keep what wampum they pick up.

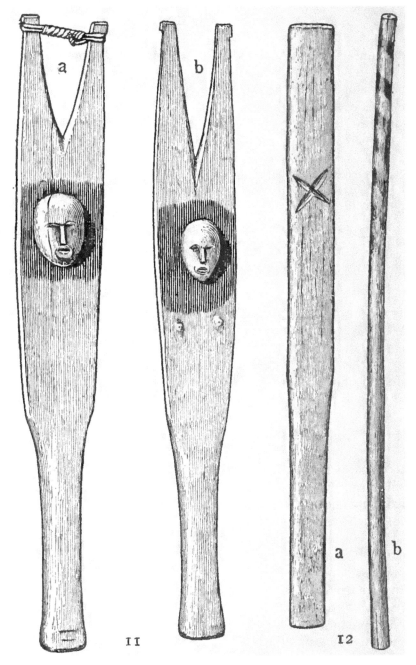

Fig. 11. — Sacred drumsticks, used at the Annual Ceremony in Oklahoma. (Length of *a*, 18.6 in.)
Fig. 12. — *a*, Plain drumstick used at the Annual Ceremony; *b*, Prayerstick. (Length of *b*, 18.9 in.)

Return of the Hunters

If the hunters are lucky and kill a deer the first day, they send one man back with it. As he approaches he fires a gun as a signal of his coming, at which the singers run into the Big House and begin to sing and beat the drum. Then everyone is happy.

In any case the hunters all return on the third day. If they have killed deer, they shoot their guns; if not, they come in very quietly. When the shots are heard, the singers hasten to their places, and, beating the drum, sing a song that is used only on such occasions. Then when the hunters arrive, they feast, and their leader announces the names of those lucky enough to kill a deer. The carcasses are skinned and hung on the deer pole (shown in frontispiece), east of the Big House, and are used in the feasts at the close of every night's meeting until the gathering disbands.

New Fire

Every night the usual program is repeated until the ninth. On this night a new fire is kindled with the sacred pump-drill called *tuɴdaʼi wähen'ji maniʼtowŭk* or "Fire maker of the Maniʼtos" (fig. 8), and the ashes of the old are carried out through the west door of the Big House, which is used only for this purpose (among the Unami), and is usually kept closed. The new fire seems to symbolize a fresh start in all the affairs of life.

Use of Carved Drumsticks

Also on the ninth night, before the singing begins, they bring out the two ancient drumsticks (*pa kŭndi'gŭn*), carved with tiny human heads, one male and one female (fig. 11), to use in place of the cruder sticks used before, which are marked only with a rude cross (fig. 12, *a*).

At this time, also, twelve prayersticks (*ma'tehi'gun*) are distributed — six plain and six striped ones (fig. 12, b) — by two of the male attendants, each with six, one man starting from each end of the Big House and proceeding in a trot to distribute the sticks while the drum is beaten, and the people, holding up their hands, cry the prayer word *"Ho-o-o!"*

Both drumsticks and prayersticks are used every night from this time on. If it so happens that the plain sticks do not fall opposite each other (or on opposite sides of the house), they must all be picked up again and redistributed. After this, those who have received a stick raise that instead of their hand, when they repeat the prayer word *"Ho-o-o!"* and carry it when they dance.

Turtle Rattles

At this time, too, all who own turtle rattles such as are used in singing the visions (fig. 9), are requested to bring them in to the meeting, when they are placed in a row on the north side, in front of the man who, as the Indians phrase it, "brought on the meeting." The backs of the turtleshells are all measured with strings of wampum, which are cut off in lengths corresponding with the lengths of the backs.

Then the owners are called to get their turtles and wampum, which is supposed to be their pay for bringing them to the meeting. As each takes up his turtle, he shakes it, and if it does not sound well, then the people laugh, and the owner, abashed, takes his property out of sight as soon as possible.

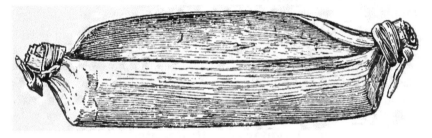

Fig. 13. — Paint-dish of bark, used at the Annual Ceremony. (Length, 2.2 in.)

Phratry Prayers

Then they call up six men, two from each of the three phratries — Turtle, Turkey, and Wolf. Each goes outside and cries the prayer word "Ho-o-o!" twelve times, holding up his left hand. When the first one returns, he is given one yard of wampum, and divides it with the other five. This is done each night until the end.

Women's Night

The twelfth night is reserved for the women to relate their visions; but before they begin, the speaker orders the attendants to burn cedar-leaves in the two fires, and the people are supposed to inhale the smoke and purify themselves. Then two women are ordered to take, one a little bark dish (a*nsipta'gŭn*) of red paint (fig. 13), the other a similar vessel of grease, and the two start from the door on the north side of the Temple and go to each person present. One dips her fingers in the paint and touches the color to the person's left cheek, while her companion similarly annoints the person's head with a little of the grease. This done, two

49

men attendants take the bark vessels and paint and grease in the same way the twelve *Mĭsi'ngw'* faces carved upon the posts of the building, also the drumsticks, the prayersticks, the deerskin drum, and the turtles. A variant has it that both bark vessels contain paint, the customs differing according to phratry.

Each woman who takes part on this night receives a share of the venison, if there is any, — the biggest and fattest buck the hunters kill, — and the attendants cook it for them at the fire outside.

Conclusion of Ceremony

Next morning the men resume the ceremony and continue until the sun is high. Two men are then appointed to close the meeting, for which each receives one yard of wampum. Their duty is to sing twelve times while the people dance about the central post, the women in a circle next to the post, the men in another circle outside that of the women. These two singers stop dancing in front of where the chief is sitting, and announce, "We will now pray twelve times." They go back to their seats and cry *"Ho-o-o!"* twelve times. Then the attendants serve the last feast. Two women then go around with wampum in a wooden bowl, giving everyone two or three beads.

Payment of Attendants

Then the attendants, three men and three women, stand in a row and receive six yards of wampum on one string, which they hold in their hands, the first in the row holding the end of the string, which stretches along from one to the other. Then the chief says: "We thank you attendants of this meeting for your kindness in sweeping our Temple for these twelve nights, and the attention and care you have given. We have heard our old parents say that, if you sweep this Meeting House twelve different times, you will sweep up to where our great Father is, as he is up in the twelfth Heaven above the earth."

The attendants then circle about the fires and go out to the cooking fireplace, where they divide the wampum, taking a yard apiece. At last, when the shadow of a person is nearly under him, that is, about noon, the speaker or chief arises, and says, "All of us kinfolk must now go out and end our meeting, which has been going on for twelve days and nights." Thereupon they all file out — men, women, and children — and form a row extending north and south, facing east, just east of the Big House, the hunters taking with them the skins of the deer they killed.

Finale

Here they all pray, or rather cry the prayer word *"Ho-o-o!"* six times standing, holding up one hand, and six times kneeling, holding up the other hand. The meeting is then ended. This is shown in the frontispiece. The deerskins are given to poor old people, who need them to make moccasins.

One informant stated that instead of crying *"Ho-o-o"* twelve times in closing the meeting, it was customary to use this word only ten times, and then cry *"Ha-a-a"* twice, completing the sacred number twelve; but such discrepancies are probably due to the variation of ritual among the three phratries before mentioned, the Turkey, the Turtle, and the Wolf. This kind of prayer was noticed by Zeisberger [45] as early as 1779, for he writes:

"At a third kind of feast ten or more tanned deer-skins are given to as many old men or women, who wrap themselves in them and stand before the house with their faces turned toward the east, praying God with a loud voice to reward their benefactors. They turn toward the east because they believe that God dwells beyond the rising of the sun. At the same time much wampum is given away. This is thrown on the ground and the young people scramble for it. Afterward it is ascertained who secured the most. This feast is called *'ngammuin,* the meaning of which they themselves are unable to give."

The suspicion that Zeisberger mistook the conclusion of the Annual Ceremony for a separate rite is strengthened by the fact that he gives its name as *"'ngammuin,"* which seems to be a form of *Ga'muing,* the modern Lenape name for their Annual Ceremony.

Payment of Officers

All the officers of the meeting receive pay in wampum for their services, except, of course, the leader — the man who has caused the meeting to be held. The speaker receives a yard for every night of the meeting; the drummers get a yard between them each night; there are also the payments to the attendants, hunters, and others, already mentioned. The attendants have other sources of profit, too, for they serve meals three times a day in the Big House to the leader of the meeting and all his near relatives, also to the speaker and the drummers.

When they have finished feasting, the leader calls the attendants to come and get their dishes and pans. Each has a cup in which he brings coffee, and the leader puts twenty-five wampum beads in each cup for every meal. Moreover, when any one in the outside camps is hungry, he may go to an *a'ckas* and obtain a meal for twenty-five wampum beads. The attendants have a table near the tent of one of the woman *a'ckas,* and here they eat.

Valuation of Wampum

For ceremonial purposes the wampum (white) is held at one cent a bead, one hundred to the dollar. Before the meeting the people give a yard or so apiece, if they are able, to show their appreciation and to be prayed for, or subscribe money for its purchase and for the other things needed at the meeting. The wampum is afterward redeemed at the same rate and is kept to use again.

Indian Comments on the Ceremony

Some explanations and remarks concerning the annual ceremony, as furnished by the Indians themselves, may prove of interest here.

Julius Fouts (or Fox), the interpreter, remarks:

"When the Delawares complete this meeting, then they claim they have worshiped everything on this earth. God gave the Powers Above authority to go around and give all the tribes some way to worship. They say these things were as if carried in a bundle, and when they come to the Delawares, last of all, there was a lot left in the bundle and they got it all — that is why the Delawares have so many different things to do in their meetings."

In explanation of the prayer word Ho-o-o, he said, "Did you ever hear that noise out in the woods, in the fall of the year? *'Ho-o-o,'* it says. What is it? It is the noise of the wind blowing in the trees. When the Delawares pray in the Big House, they raise their voices and cry *'Ho-o-o'* to God, and the Mĭsi'ngw' hears it and understands, for he is of the same nature as a tree, and there are twelve Mĭsi'ngw' carved in the Big House who will carry the prayers to the twelfth Heaven. The Indians call the Mĭsi'ngw' 'Grandfather,' because the trees were here before the Indians. The Big House is going out of use now, because only the old people have had gifts or visions of power to sing about. The children of today are not *pi'lsun,* or pure; they are reared like the whites, and the Powers Above do not speak to them any more."

Chief Charley Elkhair, or Elkire, who frequently served as speaker in the Big House, said:

"The Delaware meeting helps everybody in the world, for they pray for good crops and everything good, even wild fruits. About ten years ago the people thought they would give up holding these meetings, and the following year they had high winds and big rains, and everyone was frightened. Then grasshoppers came in swarms, but they came in the fall a little too late to get all the crops. So the people held a council and talked about the Big House again. They finally decided to resume it, before any more bad luck came; so they began the ceremonies again in the fall.

"Then it seemed as if all the trouble stopped. Of late there has been talk of again giving up the meeting, but if we do give it up we are likely to have a tornado or maybe dry weather to ruin the crops.

"Once the Delawares owned a great deal of land, but that is nearly all gone now, and the people seem to have no power to do anything. When God looks down from Heaven, he sees but very few Delaware people, and the reason for this is that they cannot follow the Meeting House ceremonies now. When I was a little boy, I heard my people say that this thing would happen just as it is happening now. You see, the young people raised during the last thirty years do not believe in the old ways. We are having good times yet, but we don't know when we shall catch it. If anything happens to us, and once really begins, we can not stop it — it will be too late. Even if they take up the meeting again — they can not do right, even when the ceremonies are going on.

"They can not accomplish anything in the Big House; they can not raise it up, because there are a lot of young folks who do not even try to do what the speaker tells them, for they do not believe in it.

"The people could get along fine, if they followed the rules of the meeting— not only the Delawares, but the other people round about. For when the Delaware prays, he prays for things that will benefit everybody; he prays for the children as well as for himself; he prays for future time. But if anything comes to destroy the world, it will be too late to think of starting the Big House then."

Penn's Account. — William Penn seems to have been the first to attempt a description of Lenape rites, for he wrote in 1683, in the same letter we have quoted before:

"Their Worship consists of two parts, sacrifice and Cantico. Their sacrifice is their first fruits...The other part of their worship is by Cantico, performed by round dances, sometimes words, sometimes songs, then shouts, two being in the middle that begin, and by singing and drumming on a board direct the chorus...They are said to lay their altar on twelve stones."

In this brief account should be noted the presence of *two* drummers; the fact that they did not use a drum, but a "board" which was probably, if Penn had taken the trouble to look more closely, a dried hide; the word cantico which resembles the modern Lenape words for "dance" — *kĭ'nĭkä* among the Unami and *kĭ'ntika* among the Minsi; and finally the use of the sacred number twelve.

Zeisberger's Account. — The earliest detailed account, however, of the great Lenape ceremonies is given by Zeisberger, [46] who, writing about 1779, says:

"Worship and sacrifices have obtained among them from the earliest times, being usages handed down from their ancestors. Though in the detail of ceremony there has been change, as the Indians are more divided now than at that time, worship and sacrifice have continued as practiced in the early days, for the Indians believe that they would draw all manner of disease and misfortune upon themselves if they omitted to observe the ancestral rites.

"In the matter of sacrifice, relationship, even though distant, is of significance, legitimate or illegitimate relationship being regarded without distinction. A sacrifice is offered by a family, with its entire relationship, once in two years. Others, even the inhabitants of other towns, are invited. Such sacrifices are commonly held in autumn, rarely in winter. As their connections are large, each Indian will have opportunity to attend more than one family sacrifice a year. The head of the family knows the time and he must provide for everything. When the head of such a family is converted, he gets into difficulty because his friends will not give him peace until he has designated someone to take his place in the arrangement of sacrificial feasts.

"Preparations for such a sacrificial feast extend through several days. The requisite number of deer and bears is calculated and the young people are sent into the woods to procure them together with the leader whose care it is to see that everything needful is provided. These hunters do not return until they have secured the amount of booty counted upon. On their return they fire a volley when near the town, march in in solemn procession and deposit the flesh in the house of sacrifice. Meantime the house has been cleared and prepared. The women have prepared fire-wood and brought in long dry reed grass, which has been strewn the entire length of the house, on both sides, for the guests to sit upon. Such a feast may continue for three or four nights, the separate sessions beginning in the afternoon and lasting until the next morning. Great kettles full of meat are boiled and bread is baked. These are served to the guests by four servants especially appointed for this service. The rule is that whatever is thus brought as a sacrifice must be eaten altogether and nothing left. A small quantity of melted fat only is poured into the fire. The bones are burnt, so that the dogs may not get any of them. After the meal the men and women dance, every rule of decency being observed. It is not a dance for pleasure or exercise, as is the ordinary dance engaged in by the Indians. One singer only performs during the dance, walking up and down, rattling a small tortoise shell filled with pebbles. He sings of the dreams the Indians have had, naming all the animals, elements and plants they hold to be spirits. None of the spirits of things that are useful to the Indians may be omitted. By worshipping all the spirits named they consider themselves to be worshipping God, who has revealed his will to them in dreams. When the first singer has finished he is followed by another. Between dances the guests may stop to eat again. There are four or five kinds of feasts, the ceremonies of which differ much from one another.

"At these feasts there are never less than four servants, to each of whom a fathom of wampum is given that they may care for all necessary things. During the three or four days they have enough to do by day and by night. They have leave, also, to secure the best of provisions, such as sugar, bilberries, molasses, eggs, butter and to sell these things at a profit to guests and spectators."

Adams' Account. — The best and, in fact, the only late account previous to his own first article [47] the writer has seen of the Annual Ceremony among the Lenape in Oklahoma, is that written by Adams, [48] which reads as follows:

"The peculiar steps which they use in this dance have caused the name 'stomp' or 'stamp' to be applied to it.

"In regard to the stomp dances of our people, we have several kinds of dances; the most important one is the 'worship dance' which is carried on in a large building called a temple, which is rectangular and ranges from 60 to 80 feet long, from 30 to 40 feet wide, and is about 10 feet high. It is built of wood with 2 doors. The main entrance is at the eastern door, and it has only a dirt floor.

"On each post is carved a human face. On the center post or one in the center of the building four faces are carved; each face is painted onehalf red and one-half black. All the people enter at the east and go out the same way. When they come in they pass to the right of the fire, and each of the three clans of the Delawares take seats next to the wall, the Turtle clan on the south, the Turkey on the west, and the Wolf on the north. In no case can any one pass between the center post and east door, but must go around the center post, even to go to the north side of the temple.

"This dance is held once each year, in the fall, and generally in October, in the full moon, and lasts not less than 12 days for each part. The tribe is divided into three clans, and each clan has to go through the same part, so the dance is sometimes 36 days long, but sometimes the second and third clans do not dance more than 6 days each.

"The Turtle clan usually lead or begin the dance. A tortoise shell, dried and beautifully polished and containing several small pebbles is placed in the southeast corner near the door in front of the first person. If he has anything to say he takes the shell and rattles it, and an answer comes from the south side of the temple from the singers, who strike on a dried deer's hide: then the party who has the tortoise shell makes an address or talk to the people, and thanks the Great Spirit for blessings, and then proceeds to dance, going to the right and around the fire, followed by all who wish to take part, and finally coming to the center post he stops there; then all the dancers shake hands and return to their seats. Then the shell is passed to the next person, who dances or passes it on, as he chooses.

"On the third day of the dance all men, both married and single, are required to keep out of the company of women for 3 days at least. They have a doorkeeper, a leader, and 2 or 3 parties who sweep the ground floor with turkey wings, and who also serve as deacons. The ashes from the fire are always taken out at the west door, and the dirt is always swept in the fire. In front of the east door outside is a high pole on which venison hangs. It is a feast dance and the deacons distribute food among the people. The officers and waiters are paid in wampum for their services.

"In no case is a dog allowed to enter the temple, and no one is allowed to laugh inside it, or in any way be rude. Each person is allowed to speak and tell his dream or dreams or to give advice. It is believed by the Delawares that every one has a guardian spirit which comes in the form of some bird, animal, or other thing, at times in dreams, and tells them what to do and what will happen. The guardian spirit is sent from the Great Spirit.

"Traditions say that 10 years before white men came to this country (America) a young man told his dream in the temple. This was on the Atlantic coast. He saw coming across the great waters a large canoe with pinions (wings) and containing strange people, and that in 10 years they would in fact come. He told this dream and predicted the arrival of the white men each year until they came and were seen by his people. Many of our people still keep up this dance, but the temple is not so large as it used to be, and the attendance now is not more than ioo persons. Any Indian of any tribe can also take part in the dance, but no white man can.

"When the dance is over all the people go out and stand in a single line from east to west with their faces to the south. Then they kneel down and pray, and then go home. We do not know the origin of the worship dance, but the old Indians claim that the Great Spirit came many years ago and instructed it and also gave them the wampum."

In spite of several inaccuracies, such as the statement that the people face *south* (instead of east) while praying after the ceremony, this account is valuable on account of the additional data it furnishes on several points of interest, especially the tradition concerning the prophecy of the coming of the whites.

Another Form of the Annual Ceremony

It appears that in former years there was, in addition to the rite just described, another form of the Annual Ceremony practised by the Lenape, before their removal to what is now Oklahoma from Kansas, where the last man to "bring in" such a meeting was John Sarcoxie, now dead.

The ceremony, which was called *MuxhatoL'zing*, seems, from the accounts given the writer by his informants, to have taken place in a similar building, and to have been similar in ritual to that just described, except that it was held for only eight days instead of twelve, and that, after the return of the hunters the skin of one of the deer they had brought in was stuffed with grass and stood up by the central post of the Big House, antlers and all, while about its neck hung a string of wampum — perhaps as a propitiatory offering.

Moreover on the morning of the last day of the ceremony a large sweathouse was built and stones heated; then about noon the men who had been reciting their visions went into it, each taking one of the hot stones with him. This privilege was not confined to the actual celebrants however, for every one blessed by a guardian spirit even if they had not sung their visions in the meeting, was entitled to carry in a stone and join them.

The entrance was then closed and water poured upon the stones; and while the steam rose and the sweathouse grew hotter and hotter the perspiring occupants prayed to their guardian spirits and recited their visions. These finished, with a shout of "There go our prayers to Those Above," the cover was suddenly snatched from the sweathouse so that the steam it had contained rose in a puff. If the steam cloud went straight up into the air it was thought that the prayers would be heard and answered, and that all was well, but if it broke and spread out the people felt that something had gone wrong, and that their prayers were of no avail.

In endeavoring to explain the presence of such variations of the Annual Ceremony, it should be remembered that the Lenape now in Oklahoma whom the writer has called for convenience "Unarm," are not really pure descendants of this tribe, but probably have a large proportion of the blood of the Unala"tko or Unalachtigo, whose dialect, according to Heckewelder, was very similar, and a smaller proportion of Minsi and even Nanticoke blood. Perhaps then the first form of Annual Ceremony described may have originally been purely Unami, and the second Unalachtigo, or Minsi, or vice versa; but later, when the remnants of these tribes became amalgamated their mixed descendants inherited both forms. The second form seems to be a variant of the rite mentioned by Zeisberger [49] who describes it as follows:

"A fifth kind of festival is held in honor of fire which the Indians regard as being their grandfather, and call *Machtuzin,* meaning 'to perspire.' A sweating-oven is built in the midst of the house of sacrifice, consisting of twelve poles each of a different species of wood. These twelve poles represent twelve Manittos, some of these being creatures, others plants. These they run into the ground, tie together at the top, bending them toward each other; these arc covered entirely with blankets, joined closely together, each person being very ready to lend his blanket, so that the whole appears like a baker's oven, high enough nearly to admit a man standing upright. After the meal of sacrifice, fire is made at the entrance of the oven and twelve large stones, about the size of human heads, are heated and placed in the oven. Then twelve Indians creep into it and remain there as long as they can bear the heat. While they are inside twelve pipes full of tobacco are thrown, one after another, upon the hot stones, which occasions a smoke almost powerful enough to suffocate those confined inside. Some one may also walk around the stones singing and offering tobacco, for tobacco is offered to fire. Usually, when the twelve men emerge from the oven, they fall down in a swoon. During this feast a whole buck-skin with the head and antlers is raised upon a pole, head and antlers resting on the pole, before which the Indians sing and pray. They deny that they pay any adoration to the buck, declaring that God alone is worshipped through this medium and is so worshipped at his will."

That this is really the same ceremony is shown not only by the details as related but by the native name of the rite, the *Machtuzin* of Zeisberger corresponding with the *MuxhatoL'zing* of the present writer.

Chapter Six - Minsi Big House Ceremonies

The following account of the great ceremonies of the Minsi, which correspond to the annual ceremony of the Unami, was obtained from Chief James Wolf, now deceased, and his nephew, Chief Nellis Timothy.

Myth of Origin

At first, it appears, the Indians did not know how to worship, so Keĕtanĭto'wĕt, the Great Manĭ'to or God, now called Pa"tŭmawas, came down and told them what to do. After following his instructions, they watched him when he ascended. He carried twelve sumach sticks in his hand, and they could see them shine far up in the air. Every now and then he dropped one, and when he dropped the twelfth he disappeared, while they heard the heavens crack like thunder behind him as he went in. After this the Lenape began to hold these meetings according to the instructions he had given them.

Number of Ceremonies

There were two of these ceremonies every year, both held in the Minsi Big House (*W'a'tekan*), which was quite similar to that of the Unami. One of these, performed about June when the wild strawberries were ripe, lasted only a single night; the other, early in winter, covered twelve days and nights. This latter corresponds to the Annual Ceremony of the Unami.

At the June ceremony fresh strawberries were made into a drink for the people, which reminds one of the Iroquois Strawberry Dance, or Dance of First Fruits, as it is sometimes called. Strawberries were dried at this time to make a drink for the Winter Ceremony.

Arrangement of the Big House

Like the Unami Big House, that of the Minsi had a large central post bearing carved faces; but, unlike that of the Unami, there was a second short post, near the central one, upon which was hung, for each ceremony, a raw fresh deerskin with the head and horns at the top. This feature, however, corresponds with the second

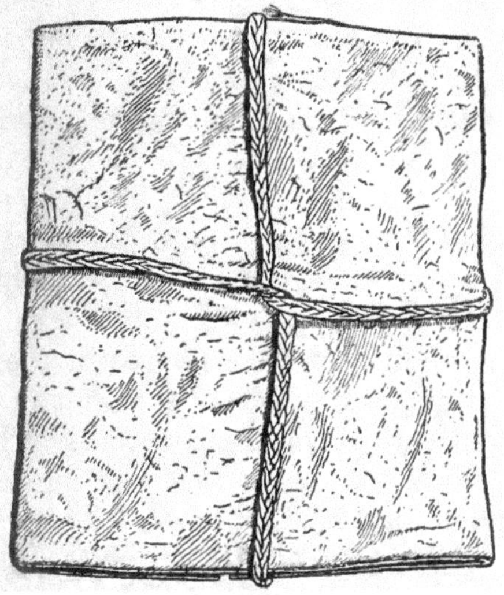

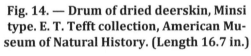

Fig. 14. — Drum of dried deerskin, Minsi type. E. T. Tefft collection, American Museum of Natural History. (Length 16.7 in.)

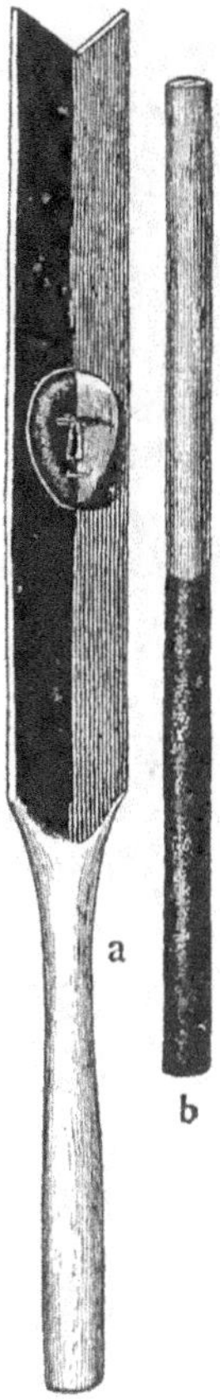

form of the Annual Ceremony noted among the Lenape in Oklahoma and also recorded by Zeisberger in Pennsylvania. Near this central post the singers sat, and beat with four carved sticks upon a dry deerhide folded into a square, in lieu of a drum (fig. 14), differing from the Unami form, which is a rolled dry deerskin upon which are tied several slats of wood (fig. 8). The drumsticks are flat, resembling those of the Unami, as each bears a face carved upon one side, but differ from them in the form of the forked end, and in width. Some, it is said, represented women, the breasts being indicated as among the Unami, but this feature does not appear in the set collected by the writer at Grand River reserve (fig. 15, *a*), which the Indians said were representative of the Minsi type.

Fig. 15. — *a*, Drumstick, Minsi type; *b*, Prayerstick. E. T. Tefft collection, American Museum of Natural History. (Length of *a*, 19 in.)

There were two poles laid along on each side from end to end of the Big House to divide the dancing place in the center from the sitting places on the side, which were covered with a special kind of leaves. Along these poles twelve little sumach sticks (fig. 15, *b*), peeled and painted, were laid for twelve people to hold in their hands, and tap on the poles in time to the music. There were also provided a turtle rattle, which was placed at the foot of the central pole; a fire-drill which Nellis Timothy thinks was worked on the "pump-drill" principle, like that of the Unami, and a lot of entirely new and unused bowls and spoons of bark. Unlike the Unami custom, both doors of the Big House were used, the people always going in at the east door and coming out at the west, and here also (like the Unami) the ashes were carried out. "The Sun and everything else goes toward the west," say the Minsi, in explanation, "even the dead when they die."

Preliminaries

The first act remembered by the informants preparatory to holding a meeting was to send to each man in the tribe who had been blessed by a "vision of power," a little stick which represented an invitation to the ceremony, the time of which the messenger gave out, before which date the people leaving their scattered homes gathered and camped about the Big House. Meanwhile hunters were sent out, appointed before, not during the meeting as among the Unami, to bring in for the Winter Ceremony, if possible, exactly twelve deer, which were cooked by four young men who served as attendants in a small separate house, built for the purpose.

Fire. — The fire was made with a fire-drill by a group of old men for use in the Big House, but, as among the Unami, none of it could be taken outside during the ceremony.

Purification. — When the two fires had been built, but before the crowd had gathered, the house was purified by the smoke of hemlock boughs thrown on the flames, and by sweeping the floor with turkey-wing fans, which cleared away both dirt and evil influences.

Opening of the Ceremony

Chiefs Speech. — The next step was for the attendants to call in all the people from their camps except the women in their menses who were not allowed to enter. When all were seated, the speaker rose and addressed those assembled in terms like the following:

"We are now gathered here, our house is purified and clean, and Pa"tŭmawas is with us, ready to hear our worship. We must thank Him for all the things that we enjoy, for He made them every one." Then he proceeded to tell the people not to drink liquor, nor to do anything wrong in the Big House or in the camp about it, and advised them to be always honest and kind and hospitable. He held virtue as something to -be followed, at the same time condemning evil, every vice that he could think of being mentioned.

The chief then gave thanks for everything he could remember, from the heavenly bodies to the animals, trees, and herbs of the earth, not forgetting corn, beans, and squashes; and prayer for successful hunting and good health for all the people. At the summer meeting he prayed for good crops also. When he had finished, bear's fat was thrown on the two fires, and the smoke rose and filled the place with its odor.

Ceremonial Drink

At this point it was customary to pass around a vessel of drink made of crushed wild strawberries, from which each person present swallowed about a spoonful, a drink made at the Summer Ceremony of fresh fruit, but in winter necessarily of berries dried for the purpose.

Recital of Visions

The first man to relate his vision (my informant did not remember whether he was the one who "brought in" the meeting or not) took up the turtle rattle from its place at the foot of the post and began to shake it rapidly, while the singers struck the drum of dry hide. He then recited the story of his vision of power, still keeping the rattle shaking, following this with his dance song, at the same time dancing and rattling the turtle-shell.

Any one who wished to dance was supposed to give wampum to the vision-teller for the privilege. Some who were well off would give him an entire string, others merely a few beads. These the vision-teller would take, when he had quite a handful, to two officers who sat in a corner of the building, whose duty it was to count the wampum, after which it was kept by the chief or leader. Sometimes if a poor person who had no wampum wished to dance, they would give him some to pay the vision-teller.

A translated example of a Minsi vision chant and dance song has already been given. When the dream-teller finished the first verse of his dance song, he exclaimed, *"E-ye-he-ye-ĕ!"* whereupon the singers took up the strain and sang the verse several times, for the benefit of those who wished to dance, omitting, however, the final exclamation, but those who had bought the privilege rose and danced where they stood, instead of circling around, as among the Unami. Each "set" ended with a whoop, *"kwi!"*.

When the vision-teller finished dancing, he went around the house and shook hands with everyone; then the turtle rattle was passed to another man who had been blessed with a vision, and so on, until all those qualified, who wished to recite their visions, had done so.

Other Features

The Prayer Cry. — From time to time during the night the prayer cry *"Ho-o-o!"* was repeated twelve times, and the twelfth cry, they say, was heard by the Great Manĭ'to.

Feast. — The people were accustomed to eat a light supper before going into the meeting; then about midnight the four attendants carried around baskets with boiled meat and corn bread, and in the morning, before leaving the Big House, a regular feast of venison was served in new bark bowls and eaten with new bark spoons especially made for the purpose.

Final Address. — Before the meeting closed, the speaker again addressed the people, telling them to do right, and prayed that the hunters about to leave for the winter hunt might be successful, and that all might live to meet again.

Conclusion of Rites

In the morning after the ceremonies in the Big House were finished, the people filed out through the west door, circled about the building, and lined up, facing eastward, to the east of it. Then they raised their hands and cried *"Ho-o-o!"* twelve times, and the twelfth time, it is said, their cry reached Heaven.

In comparing this form of the Annual Ceremony with that of the Oklahoma Lenape the most noticeable difference is that here no masked impersonator of Mĭsinghâli'kŭn was seen in or about the Big House, the Masks among the Minsi, as with the Iroquois, constituting a society with its own separate rites.

Grand River Version

Such was the version of the great ceremonies given the writer by the Minsi of Munceytown, Ontario, which is similar to, but more detailed in parts than, the account previously obtained from the Delawares of Grand River reserve, published by the writer in the *American Anthropologist* [50] which we will reproduce here. It will be noticed that this description gives fuller information in some places where the first is deficient; so that between this and the preceding account, a good general idea of the Minsi form of the ceremony can be reconstructed. It reads:

"In the old religious ceremonies of the Delawares at Grand River a very peculiar drum was used, a dry skin folded in rectangular form and beaten with four sticks, each bearing a tiny human head carved in relief (fig. 15, *a*). I secured the set of four original sticks from Michael Anthony (*Nankŭma'oxa*), and employed him to make me a reproduction of the drum (fig. 14) as the original had been destroyed. This he did, and in addition made six painted sticks (fig. 15, *b*) also used in the ceremony. The description of how these articles were used, pieced together from several Indian accounts, may prove of interest here.

"It appears that the Delawares of Six Nations Reserve formerly held what was known as a 'General Thanksgiving' ceremony called in Lenape *Gitctla'kan*, twice a year, once in the spring and again in the fall. At these times it was customary to meet in the Cayuga long-house, borrowed for the occasion. At a certain point in the proceedings (I shall not attempt a consecutive description from hearsay testimony) a man stood up and recited, in a rythmical sing-song tone, his dream — the vision of power seen by him in his youth. Na'nkŭma'oxa remembered how one old man was accustomed to tell about a duck, half black and half white, which had appeared to him. Between the verses of the dream four musicians kneeling at the drum (*pw'awahe'gŭn*) began a plaintive song, beating time with the carved sticks (*pw'awake'gŭnŭk*). As they sang, the reciter swayed his body to and fro, while a group of dancers gathered on the floor behind him danced with a sidewise step. Before the ceremony, poles were laid lengthwise along both sides of the council house, and against these, at intervals, three on a side, the painted sticks, called *mkääki'gŭn*, were laid. If anyone in the crowd felt 'especially happy' he was privileged to strike with one of these sticks upon one of the poles in time to the music. The carved heads on the drumsticks meant that human beings were giving thanks; the lengthwise painting of the sticks, half black and half red, implied that men and women were together in thanksgiving, the black representing the warriors, the red the women. The fork at the striking end of the sticks was to give a sharper sound. The dyes for producing the colors were made by boiling bark, the black being soft maple (*sexi'kiminsi*), and the red, red alder bark (*wito"pi*).

"In another part of the same ceremony wampum was used in the form of strings and bunches, both of which were represented in my collection from the Delawares. At least thirteen of the strings were used, each one made different by different combinations of the white and purple beads. These thirteen, it is said, represented respectively (1) Earth; (2) Plants; (3) Streams and Waters; (4) Corn, Beans, and Vegetables; (5) Wild Birds and Beasts; (6) Winds; (7) Sun; (8) Moon; (9) Sky; (10) Stars; (11) Thunder and Rain; (12) Spirits; and (13) Great Spirit. At the ceremony these strings were laid upon a bench before a speaker, who picked them up one

63

by one as he made his address, each string reminding him of one part of his speech. He began, my informant told me, by explaining that the Great Spirit had made all things — the earth, plants, streams, and waters — everything. Having thus enumerated all the things represented by the wampum, he proceeded to speak to each of the remaining twelve directly, holding the appropriate string in his hand. Thus he gave thanks to the Earth for the benefits it gives to man, and prayed that its blessings might continue; then thanked in the same way the Plants, the Streams and Waters, the Winds; the Corn, Beans, and Vegetables — each one in turn. As he finished each string he handed it to an attendant, who laid it aside. When his long speech or prayer was finished, he announced, 'We will now enjoy ourselves,' and selected a man to distribute little bunches of wampum, three beads in each, which served as invitations to join in the dancing that followed. These bunches were delivered only to a certain number of those known to be 'sober and honest' among the crowd in the long-house. If any person wishing to dance failed to get invitation wampum, it was his privilege to ask for one of the bunches, which was given him if he was considered qualified. The first man receiving wampum arose first; then the others, until the dancers were all on the floor. It is said that this dance, which sometimes lasted all night, did not circle around like most of the Iroquois dances, but each performer remained in about the same spot. "I was told that in this dance a small rattle without a handle and made of turtle-shell was used, probably like the box-turtle rattle still used in the annual Planting Dance by the Seneca and Cayuga."

Waubuno's Version

The only extended account in print, known to the writer, of the great ceremonies of the Minsi, beside his own, quoted above, is that furnished by John Wampum, known as Chief Waubuno, [51] which reads as follows:

"They kept annual feasts: — ...a feast of first fruits which they do not permit themselves to taste until they have made an offering of them to the mani-tu-oo-al, or gods; ...There is one of the greatest sacrifice offerings of our forefathers every six months for cleansing themselves from sin; they will have twelve deers to be consumed in one day and night. At the great feast of the offerings of the first fruits of the earth, which feast the Delawares or Munceys hold annually, they brought a little of all that they raised, such as Indian corn, or hweisk-queem, potatoes, beans, pumpkins, squashes, together with the deer. The Indian women were busily engaged in cooking their provisions, previous to the commencement of their exercises. They invited all strangers into a long pagan temple prepared for such purposes, there is a door at each end — one opening to the east, and one opening to the west. On entering, they with all the Indians were seated on the ground around two fires; in the center of the temple was a large post, around which was suspended a number of deer skins, and wampum is kept buried at the foot of this post. Near the post sat two Indian singers, each with a large bundle of undressed deer skins which served as drums. There were two young men appointed to watch the doors and keep the fires burning, the doors being closed. Each of the young men brought an armful of hemlock boughs, which being thrown on the fires smothered them and caused a great smoke. In order that the smoke might fill every corner of the temple, each man waved his blanket over the fire; this was done with the idea of purifying the temple and driving out the evil spirits. After the smoke had subsided, the master of ceremonies, an old chief, rose and began to rattle a turtle shell he had in his hand. He delivered a speech to the people telling them the object of the meeting was to thank the great spirit for the growth and ripening of the corn. When he finished his speech he began to dance, sing and rattle the shell, the two singers joining in, beating on their skins. When he took his seat he handed the shell to the next person, who performed in the same way, thus it went from one to the other all night. The purport of their speeches was to recount the mercies of the Great Spirit to them during the past year, and telling any remarkable dreams that they had had. In the course of the night a number of them went out the west door, making a wailing noise to the moon, and came in again the east door. In the morning the meat and soup were divided amongst the people.

"These feasts often lasted twelve days and twelve nights, and the Indians call it nee-shawneechk-togho-quanoo-maun, or ween-da-muchteen. No drinking or improper conduct is allowed. The utmost solemnity prevails."

Chapter Seven - The Mĭsi'ng$_w$' or Mask

The Minsi version of the myth explaining the origin of their great ceremonies has been already related, but not that of the Unami, for the latter, which concerns itself with the origin of the Unami rites as now practised, is so intimately interwoven with the story of the Mĭsi'ng$_w$' or mask (fig. 1), that it was thought best to place it in the chapter devoted to that curious being, with whose position in the Lenape pantheon, recorded history, and activities in the Annual Ceremony, we have already become acquainted.

The myth is therefore presented herewith, as related by Chief Charley Elkhair, the Lenape master of ceremonies, with only such additions as later questioning brought forth.

Origin of the Mask, and of the Big House

This is the way the Lenape found out that there is a living Mĭsinghâ-li'kŭn above us. Many years ago, when the Delawares lived in the East, there were three boys who were not treated very well. Their relatives did not take care of them, and it seemed as if it made no difference whether the children died or not. These boys were out in the woods thinking about their troubles, when they saw the Mĭsinghâli'kŭn or Living Solid Face. He came and spoke to them, and gave them strength so that nothing could hurt them again. To one of these boys he said, "You come along with me and I will show you the country I come from." So he took the boy up in the air to the place whence he came, which is rocky mountains above us, reaching out from the north and extending toward the south. It is not the place where people go when they die, for it is not very far from this earth. A long time ago people could see this country of Mĭsinghâli'kŭn, but none can see it now.

While he was showing the boy his country, the Mĭsinghâli'kŭn promised him that he would become stout and strong, and would have the power to get anything he wished. Then he brought the boy back.

Afterward, when the boy grew up and went hunting, he used to see the Mĭsinghâli'kŭn riding a buck around among the other deer, herding them together. Thus it happened that there were three men in the tribe, who knew that there is a Mĭsinghâli'kŭn, because they had seen him with their own eyes.

The Delawares had always kept a Big House (*xi'ngwikan*) to worship in, but in those days it was built entirely of bark and had no faces of the Mĭsi'ngwᵘ' carved upon the posts as it has now. Here they used to sing about their dreams (visions of power); but some time after the three boys talked with the Misinghali'kun, the people gave up this worship, and for ten years had none. Then there came a great earthquake, which lasted twelve months and gave great trouble to the Lenape. It came because they had abandoned the worship their fathers had taught them. In those times the tribe lived in towns, not scattered about the country as they are now, and in one of these towns a chief had a big bark house, and here the people met to worship, hoping to stop the earthquake, while they were building a new Big House. When it was finished, they began to worship there, and sang and prayed all winter for relief. After spring came, they were holding a meeting one night when they heard the Mĭsinghâli'kŭn making a noise, *"Hoɴ-hoɴ-hoɴ,"* right east of the Big House. The chief, who did not know what was making the noise, called for somebody to go and see what it was. Then these three men offered to go, because, as they said, they knew what was making the noise and could find out what he wanted. So they went out and found Mĭsinghâli'kŭn, and asked him what he wanted. He answered:

"Go back and tell the others to stop holding meetings and attend to their crops. Do not meet again until fall, when I will come and live with you, and help in the Big House. You must take wood and carve a face

(Mĭsi'ngwʻ) just like mine, painted half black and half red, as mine is, and I will put my power in it, so that it will do what you ask. When the man who takes my part puts the face on, I will be there, and this is how I will live among you. This man must carry a turtle rattle and a stick, just as I do now." Then he told them how to lix the twelve carved faces on the posts of the Big House, and the faces on the drumsticks, and taught them how to hold the ceremony.

Then he said:

"You must also give me hominy every year in the spring. I take care of the deer and other game, that is what I am for. Wherever you build the Big House, I will keep the deer close by, so that you can get them when you need them.

"Never give up the Big House. If you do, there will be another earthquake, or something else just as bad.

"The earthquake stopped that time; that is why the Delawares have kept the Mĭsi'ngwʻ and the Big House ever since. The Mask is left in charge of some family who will take good care of it, and burn Indian tobacco for it from time to time."

It will be seen that, according to the above tradition, the Mĭsi'ngwʻ was, first of all, a personal helper, or guardian Spirit, that afterward became more or less of a tribal deity, and that his cult became engrafted on the Annual Ceremony among the Unami, the rites of which were already ancient among them. That this engrafting really took place seems possible from the fact that among the Minsi there were no masked performers at the Big House ceremonies, and that, while the central post of the temple was provided with carved faces, the masks had an entirely different function among this people. The innovation, if it took place at all, must have been before Brainerd's [52] time, however, for, as related in our first chapter, he found the Mĭsi'ngwʻ and Big House in use, as among the Unami today, as early as May, 1745, while traveling among the Delawares living at that time on Susquehanna river.

Mĭsi'ngwʻ Dance

Besides the part taken by the Mĭsi'ngwʻ in the Annual Ceremony, he has certain rites peculiar to himself which were held every spring. As the Indians put it:

"When spring comes, the Delawares are glad, and they are thankful that their helper, the Mĭsi'ngwʻ is still among them. For this reason they give a feast and dance to make him happy too."

Notification. — So at the time of the full moon (about May), the keeper of the mask gives another Indian a yard of wampum to ride around to all the Delaware houses, wearing the mask and bearskin costume (pl. 11) to let the people know that the time for the Mĭsi'ngw' dance (Misingki' 'nika) is at hand. The Mĭsi'ngw' rides horseback, and another man, also mounted, follows him to see that he comes to no harm. At each house the impersonator dismounts and enters, making known his errand by signs, but saying only "Hon-hon-hon" and everywhere they give him tobacco, which he puts in his sack. At this time the people frighten disobedient children with the threat that, unless they behave, the Mĭsi'ngw' will carry them away in a sack full of snakes.

Preparations. — The dance-ground customarily used for this purpose has meanwhile been put in order, a cleared place in the woods selected for good shade and pleasant surroundings, and the logs which serve as seats arranged to form the rectangle within which the dance takes place. A great pot of hominy is also prepared; this constitutes the main dish of the feast.

The Ceremony. — When the people have gathered on the night appointed, and the impersonator has returned from the bushes where he retired to dress, wearing the mask and bearskin suit (pi. 11), the speaker addresses the people and relates the origin of the dance, then addressing the Mĭsi'ngw' says, "Take care of us while we are dancing, so that everything goes smoothly." Then they have a dance in which the Mĭsi'ngw' joins, but he dances around the outside of the circle of people, not with them. When they have finished, he dances twelve changes alone, which occupies the time until morning. When daylight appears, the hominy is brought out and everyone eats, including the Mĭsi'ngw', after which the speaker says, "Now we have eaten with our Mĭsi'ngw'. We will have this dance again next spring." The people then disperse to their homes, the Misi'ngw' is put away and the impersonator paid a yard of wampum for his dancing. At this dance the singers keep time by striking with sticks on a dry deer-hide rolled over and stuffed with dried grass, very similar to the "drum" used in the Big House.

Adams' Account. — The only account the writer has seen of this ceremony is that of Adams', [53] the chief inaccuracy of which is the statement that the dance is "only for amusement." It furnishes, however, several additions to our knowledge of the "Solid Face." It is as follows:

"Messingq or Solid Face Dance or Devil Dance. — The principal leader in this dance is the Messingq, an Indian, who is dressed in a bearskin robe with a wooden face, one-half red and one-half black. He has a large bearskin pouch and carries a stick in one hand and a tortoise shell rattle in the other. He is a very active person. The dance is only for amusement, and men and women join in it. A large place is cleared in the woods, and the ground is swept clean and a fire built in the center. Across the fire and inside of the ring is a long hickory pole supported at each end by wooden forks set in the ground. On

68

the east of this pole the singers stand; on the west end is a venison or deer, which is roasted. About daylight, when the dance is nearly over, all the dancers eat of the venison. They have a dried deer hide stretched over some hickory poles, and standing around it beat on the hide and sing. The dancers proceed around the fire to the right, the women on the inside next to the fire. After the dance is under headway the Messingq comes from the darkness, jumps over the dancers, and dances between the other dancers and the fire. He makes some funny and queer gestures, kicks the fire, and then departs. The Messingq is never allowed to talk, but frequently he visits the. people at their homes. He is a terror to little children, and when he comes to a house or tent the man of the house usually gives him a piece of tobacco, which the Messingq smells and puts in his big pouch, after which he turns around and kicks back toward the giver which means 'thank you,' and departs. He never thinks of climbing a fence, but jumps over it every time that one is in his way. The Devil dance is what the white men call it, but the Delawares call it the Messingq, or 'solid face' dance. The Messingq does not represent an evil spirit, but is always considered a peacemaker. I suppose that it is from his hideous appearance that white men call him the devil."

Other Functions of Mĭsi'ngw‘

The Mĭsi'ngw‘ the Indians claim, "takes care of the children," as well as of the deer, for as before related if any Delaware has a child who is weak, sickly, or disobedient, he sends for the Mĭsi'ngw‘ and asks him to "attend to" his child, On his arrival it does not take the impersonator long to frighten the weakness, sickness, or laziness out of such children, so that "afterward they are well and strong, and whenever they are told to do a thing, they lose no time in obeying." This is the only trace of the doctoring function of the mask found among the Unami.

When the keeper of the Mĭsi'ngw‘ burns tobacco for him and asks for good luck in hunting, "it turns out that way every time;" and the Lenape say moreover that if anyone loses horses or cattle, either strayed away or stolen, he can go to the keeper of the Mĭsi'ngw‘ with some tobacco as a gift and get them back. He explains his errand to the keeper, who in turn informs the Mĭsi'ngw‘ that they want him to look for the horses or cattle. The loser then goes back home, and after a few days the missing animals return, driven back by the Mĭsi'ngw‘ who if they had been tied or hobbled by the thieves, frightened them until they broke away and came home. When the Big House meeting is held in the fall, the Mĭsi'ngw‘ as before related, is seen going around among the tents of the Delawares assembled, and in and out of the Big House, always coming from the woods, where the impersonator has a place to change his clothes. The Indians say:

"He helps the people with their hunting, and also helps in the Big House while the ceremonies are in progress. If he finds anyone there who has not done right, he informs the three guards of the meeting, who take that person and put him out. In all these ways the Mĭsi'ngw' helps the Delawares."

Masks of the Minsi

The Minsi Mizi'nk (cognate with the Unami *Mĭsi'ngw'*) was a mask made of wood with copper or brass eyes and a crooked nose, according to my informants at Munceytown; and judging by Peter Jones' drawings (pl. III) they were provided also with hair, tufts of feathers, and jingling copper cones or deer-hoofs. The Mizink at Grand river was of Minsi type, judging by the specimen obtained by the writer (fig. 4).

Such masks were made to represent Mizinkhali'kun, who was "something like a person, but different from the Indians, and was powerful. They saw him first among the rocks on a hill, and he spoke to them and told them what to do to get his power. When a man put on a Mizink he received the power of this person or spirit; he could even see behind him, and could cure diseases."

The Mask Society. — The men who owned these masks formed a kind of society which Nellis Timothy says originally had twelve members, but which, before it disbanded, dwindled to about five. Sometimes only two appeared in costume.

The society had a meeting-house of its own where its dances, *Mizinkĭ'ntĭka,* were held, for, unlike the Unami custom, no Mizink ever appeared in the Big House. The members appeared wearing their masks and clad in rough bearskin and deerskin costumes, while some, at least, where provided with a turtle-shell rattle which they would rub on a long pole, crying *"On-on-on!"* the while.

Ceremonies. — While no consecutive account of their ceremonies is now remembered, it was said that they sometimes put down their rattles, heaped up the ashes from the two fires, then threw the ashes all over the house to prevent the people assembled from having disease.

Should any sick person appear, he or she would be especially treated with ashes. Sometimes the performers would pick up live coals and throw them about, frightening the people. At other times the whole company of them would go around to the different houses begging for tobacco, and would dance in any house where someone was willing to sing for them.

Nothing was said among the Minsi about the Mizink bringing back stray stock or driving deer, characteristic attributes of the Mask Being of the

Unami. The writer obtained but one mask among the Canadian Lenape, and this was from the Grand River band (fig. 4); it has been described by him [54] in the following words:

"But one mask (*mizink*) was obtained. It differed from those of the Iroquois chiefly in being cruder, and also in decoration, the lines being burnt into the wood instead of being painted or carved. The original use of the mask had to do, in part at least, with healing the sick, but Isaac Montour (*Kapyŭ'hŭm*), from whom I bought it, failed to make himself clear as to the details."

It will be seen that the Minsi beliefs and practices noted above resemble those of the False Face Company of the Iroquois tribes much more than they do the customs connected with Mĭsi'ngwʻ among the Unami.

In fact, a vague tradition exists to the effect that the False Face Company of the Cayuga once put a stop to an epidemic of cholera among the Minsi. While this was not given to account for the origin of the society among the Minsi, it at least shows that they were familiar with the Iroquois practices in this line.

Chapter Eight - Minor Ceremonies

The Doll Being

The Doll Being, called by the Unami *O''das* and by the Minsi Nani'tis, has been already mentioned as a minor Lenape deity, and it now remains only to relate the ceremonies and beliefs connected with it, beginning with the myth accounting for its origin.

Myth of Origin

Long ago, the Lenape say, some children, playing with sticks, decided to cut faces upon them, and were then very much surprised to notice that the little dolls which they had thus made seemed to have life. Their parents made them throw the dolls away when they discovered this, and most of the children soon forgot what had happened. One little girl, however, grieved for her doll; it bothered her all the time, and finally she began to dream of it every night. Then she told her parents of her trouble, and they realized that they should not have compelled her to throw the doll away. One night the doll appeared to the child and spoke to her, saying, "Find me and keep me always, and you and your family will ever enjoy good health. You must give me new clothing and hold a dance for me every spring," and then told her exactly what to do. The girl reported this to her parents, who immediately looked for the doll and found it, then dressed it, made some hominy, killed a deer, and held a dance in its honor as they were instructed, and this rite has been continued to the present day.

Preparations for the Ceremony

When the family owning a doll of this kind is ready to conduct the Doll Dance (*O"das-kĭ'nĭkä*), they select two men to gather firewood and to clean up the dance-ground used every year, and to engage a speaker and two singers, paying each of them with a yard of wampum. The dance-ground is square, similar to that used for the *Mĭsi'ngw'* dance, with logs ranged about for seats, in some pleasant place out in the woods. A hunter is then selected, who calls on several to help him get a deer, which, when brought in, is hung on poles prepared for it at the dance-ground, where it remains over night. The next morning they cook the deer and a kettle of hominy, and are then ready for the ceremony.

The Doll Dance

About the middle of the afternoon the speaker rises and addresses the people, telling them the story of the doll's origin and explaining its function; then he addresses the doll, which has now been fastened on a pole, calling it "grandmother" and notifying it that they are about to hold a dance in its honor, at the same time asking it to insure good health to the family of its owner. When he finishes, the dance leader, who should be a relative of the family owning it, takes the doll on its pole, and then, as the drummers sitting in the center of the dance-ground begin to strike the dry hide stuffed with grass that serves as a drum, and to sing the song of the Doll dance, he commences to dance, circling round the drummers, still carrying the doll, the people falling in behind him, forming two circles, the men inside, next to the drummers, and the women outside. When the leader finishes his "set," he passes the doll pole to the man behind him, who repeats the process, and so on until the men dancers have carried it six times, when it is transferred to the women, who, in their turn, dance six sets, making twelve in all, the Lenape sacred number.

The twelve sets, or "changes," lengthen the ceremony far into the night, and this necessitates a large fire to give light. This is built near the center of the danceground. Sometimes, if the crowd in attendance is large, two such fires are built. Between the changes the doll pole is stuck into the ground near the fire. When the twelfth set is finished, the speaker announces, "The Doll Dance is over," and the feast of hominy and venison is served to everyone. Then the speaker says: "If you want to dance the rest of the night, you may do so, for many of you have come a long way from home and should have a chance for more enjoyment. We will hold another Doll Dance next year." Then they put the doll away and amuse themselves with various social dances until morning.

"Nahneetis The Guardian of Health"
(E. T. Tefft Collection, American Museum of Natural History) (Plate VIII.)

Minsi Doll Ceremony

Among the Minsi the beliefs concerning the Doll Being were similar, but differed in detail. As to origin, Wolf told the writer that one time a man lay ill, likely to die, and his family called in a medicine-man, or "witch-doctor." The shaman finally announced that the family must make one of these dolls and care for it, and that the sick man would then get well. This was done, and the doctor's prediction being realized, the Minsi have ever since made and used these dolls, called in their dialect *nani'tĭs,* which were transmitted from parents to children. Wolf's own mother had one, carved out of wood in the form of a person, with a woman's dress and moccasins (for as a rule they represent women); and she always cared for it religiously, in the belief that if well treated it would protect the family and give them good health, but if neglected, someone would surely die. Every year, in the fall, when the deer are in their best condition, Wolf's mother held a dance for it, called "Feeding the Nani'tĭs;" but she did more than feed it: she put new clothes on it, three sets, and new moccasins every year. She believed that the image sometimes went about of its own accord, although she kept it carefully in a box, for the old dresses always seemed worn at the bottom and soiled, and she found burrs clinging to them when she went to put new clothes on "Nani'tĭs."

She hired a man especially to hunt a yearling doe for the ceremony, which took place in her own dwelling. The details are lost, but it is remembered that a man beat a little drum and sang while she, as owner, danced around, carrying the doll in her hands, followed by such of the other women present as wished to participate. Said Wolf, "The Nani'tĭs helped the Indians, that's why they fed it."

An Old Minsi "Doll." — The writer was able to obtain but one old specimen of this type (pl. viii), which was procured at the Grand River reserve, Ontario, for the E. T. Tefft collection, now in the American Museum of Natural History, and was described in the writer's article, 55 before cited, as follows:

"Perhaps the most interesting Delaware specimen of all is the little wooden image, about eight inches high, bought of Dr. Jones, which his father, Rev. Peter Jones, described and illustrated in his book under the name 'Nahneetis, the Guardian of Health.' He says:

"'I have in my possession two family gods. One is called Pabookowaih — the god that crushes or breaks down diseases. The other is a goddess named Nahneetis, the guardian of health. This goddess was delivered up to me by Eunice Hank, a Muncey Indian woman, who with her friends used to worship it in their sacred dances, making a feast to it every year, when a fat doe was sacrificed as an offering, and many presents were given by the friends assembled. She told me she was now restored to worship the Christian's God, and therefore had no further use for it.'

"There can be no doubt in this case concerning the identity of this specimen with the one illustrated in the book quoted. It will be noticed however by those who are familiar with Peter Jones' illustration that Nahneetis, like many humans, has lost her hair in her old age. An interesting feature of the specimen is the primitive skirt, which is made apparently by belting a blanket-like bit of cloth, bound at the edges, around Nahneetis' waist. A vestige of this method of making a skirt survives, I think, in the form of the beaded strip running up one of the vertical seams of the more modern Indian skirt, among both the Delawares and the Iroquois."

The writer afterward found such skirts still in use among the Lenape in Oklahoma (pl. I, *b*).

An Early Account of Nani'tĭs. — Another early account of the Nani'tĭs among the Minsi may be found in the Wisconsin Historical Collections, among the documents relating to the Stockbridge Mission, written by the Rev. Cutting Marsh. 56 It reads as follows:

"Nov. 6th [1839]. A Munsee Indian who came to this place over a year previous from Canada called upon me with an interpreter in order to give up a family idol. This man whose name is Big-Deer is upwards of 50 years of age, and since removing to this place, thro' the influence of this family above mentioned has attended meetings constantly and gives some evidence of a change of heart.

"The history of this idol was very interesting. He said that his mother gave it to him before her death which occurred about 29 years ago, and that he had worshipped it until within a few years when he heard about Jesus Christ, but had never given it up before. 'Now he says I wish to give it up and follow the Lord Jesus Christ, and I give this idol to you and you may do what you are a mind to with it.' It was indeed not only a 'shameful thing,' but a horribly looking object about the size of a common doll; fantastically arrayed in Indian costume and nearly covered with silver broaches and trinkets; and whilst retained as an object of worship was kept wrapped up in some 20 envelopments of broad-cloth trimmed with scarlet ribbon. They called it their ' Mother,' it is more than a hundred years old, and its late possessor was the fourth generation which had worshipped it. The season for worshipping it was in the fall after a hunt when they made a feast to it and danced around it. 'If they did not do this every fall they said, that is, make the feast &c. it would be angry and destroy them by some dreadful sickness.' It was therefore an object of fear or dread with them, but not one of love and compassion."

Bear Ceremony

We will now consider two ceremonies of the Unami which are based on animal cults which show a considerable similarity not only in their traditional origin, but also in their ritual.

The more important seems to be the one called *Papasokwi"lŭn,* which, although no part of a bear appears in its rites as practised within recent years, was evidently a Bear ceremony in the days when these animals were abundant. It also exhibits some features suggesting the Annual Ceremony before described, but there is no Mĭsi'ngw', and there are many other important differences.

Traditional Origin

The Indians say that a cub bear, kept as a pet by a Lenape family long ago, became a great playmate of one of the little sons of the family, but finally grew so large that the child's parents decided to get rid of it; so they tied a little bag of tobacco around its neck and told it to go away. This it did, but the little boy, its playmate, soon fell ill, and his parents searched in vain for a cure. After a long while one of the Indian doctors told his parents that if they would hold a ceremony of this kind and repeat it every two years, the child would recover and would keep his health. This was done; the boy recovered, and his family, who belong to the Wolf phratry, have continued to practise the rites ever since, believing that it preserves their health.

Preparations

This ceremony required a special house, which was made new for it every two years, so the first thing the family did, when the time approached, was to find a number of men, each of whom was paid a yard of wampum to cut forks and poles and erect the building. This was made by setting up a frame of poles in the form of a Big House, but smaller, only seven paces wide and fifteen paces long, then covering the top with brush and piling brush at the sides. Then to the east of the house a pole was erected, upon which to hang the meat for the feast, which, in old times, had to be a bear; but when bears became scarce a black hog was substituted, and of late a hog of any color has been used. The building finished, the hog was killed, and, having been hung on the pole overnight, was taken into the house the next day, quartered, singed on a fire that had been built inside, then carried out again, cut up, and cooked, all except the loose fat, which was kept for a special purpose, as will appear later. When done, the meat was kept in large baskets, with the exception of the head, which, having been cooked whole, was placed in a large bowl with two of the animal's ribs in its mouth.

The Rites

When night came, the leader entered the brush house, taking with him a turtle rattle similar to that used in the Annual Ceremony, followed by the men who were to participate (no women being allowed), and then made a speech, telling of the men who had "brought in" this meeting, and explaining its origin, but making no prayers to the Great Spirit or to any of the *maní'towŭk*, his helpers. He then threw half of the hog-fat upon the fire, and placed a string of wampum around his own neck. At this juncture the cook brought him the hog's head in its bowl, and then, first announcing, "I am now going to carry the head around," the leader began to chant and to walk about the house, making false motions to everyone as if to give him the head, then withdrawing it and proceeding to the next. The burden of the chant, the Indians say, was "what his dream helper told him," very much as in the Big House, but here the people kept time to his chant orally, saying *"Hu-hu-hu!"* until he stopped. The informant does not know who, if any one, shook the rattle. Probably it was employed by the singers after the burning of the head. After making the circuit twice, the leader hung his string of wampum upon some old man of the Turkey phratry who had a "vision of power," who took the head and made his rounds in the same way. He finally cut off the ears of the head, pulled the ribs from its mouth, and threw it into the fire, bowl and all. The meat was then distributed to everyone, whereupon the floor was open to any man who wished to sing an account of his vision. A bucket of prepared drink was placed at each end of the house for the refreshment of such singers, but the head, of course, was gone. When the songs were finished, the remainder of the fat, and finally the broth in which the meat had been cooked, were thrown upon the fire, and in conclusion, six women were called in and instructed to go out and give six times the prayer cry, *"Ho-o-o!"*

Perhaps the following ceremony noted by Zeisberger [57] may have been of this kind:

"A fourth kind of feast is held in honor of a certain voracious spirit, who, according to their opinions, is never satisfied. The guests are, therefore, obliged to eat all the bear's flesh and drink the melted fat. Though indigestion and vomiting may result they must continue and npt leave anything."

Otter Ceremony

Similar to the Bear ceremony in many ways, both in traditional origin and in rites, was the observance called *A"tcigamu'Ltin*, said to mean "compulsory hog-eating," held to propitiate the Otter spirit, a cult whose paraphernalia the writer was fortunate enough to collect for the Museum of the American Indian, Heye Foundation.

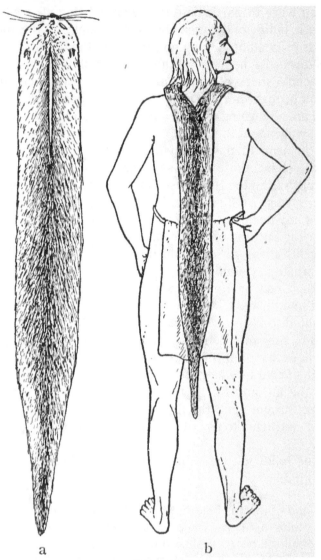

Fig. 16. — *a*, Regalia of otter-skin used in the Otter Rite; *b*, Regalia as worn. (Length of *a*, 56.5 in.)

Myth of Origin

Many years ago, so runs the story, a little girl about ten years of age was given a young otter for a pet, and this she kept and cared for until it was well grown. About this time she began to feel that she should keep him no longer, for she had come to realize that he was *pi'lsun,* meaning "pure" or "sacred," and, like all wild things, belonged to the Powers Above. The old people told her what she must do, so she took her otter down to the creek, and, first tying a little bag of tobacco on his neck, said to him: "Now I shall set you free. I have raised you and cared for you until now you are full grown. Go, then, and follow the ways of your kind."

The otter disappeared into the waters, and the little girl returned to her home, feeling that she had done well. But before a year had passed, a sickness came upon her, which the Indian doctors told her was caused by her pet otter, which wanted something to eat. The only way for the child to get well, they said, was for her to have a hog killed and cooked, and then to invite* a number of men to eat it all, in the name of the otter. This was done, and when the men finished eating the hog and the soup, they said that the girl would recover, and so she did. For this ceremony they took an otter-skin (fig. 16, *a*) to represent the girl's pet, which was used every two years, and when the owner died was passed to the oldest survivor of the family which owned it, and kept in the belief that it would benefit the health of all of them. It was the only one of its kind in the tribe, and is called "*Kunu*n'*xäs*."

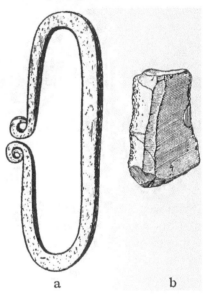

a   b

Fig. 17. Flint and steel used in the Otter Rite. (Length of *a*, 3 in.)

The Ceremony

The exact details and order of the ceremony were not remembered by our informant, but it was certain that the family in question "fed the otter" every two years in the spring, that being the time of year when the little girl had been taken ill. Everyone was invited, men and women, and a man was selected to cook the hog, and another to supply wood and to cut the poles for swinging the kettle, both of whom were paid with a yard of wampum. The fire was kindled with a special flint-and-steel always kept with the outfit (fig. 17).

It will be observed that the otter-skin has a slit down the middle of the neck, through which the owner thrust his head in such manner that the otter's nose lay under the wearer's chin, while its body and tail hung down his back. Wearing the skin in this manner (fig. 16, *b*), himself impersonating the original otter, the owner would open the ceremony by walking about the fire, chanting and shaking the turtle rattle (fig. 18), which resembles those used in the Big House, while the audience kept time to his song by uttering *"Hu-hu-hu-hu!"* The nature of the song the writer was unable to learn, but, like the chants of the Bear Ceremony, it probably was concerned with the singer's "dream helper." When he had finished, another man put on the skin and took up the chant, and so on until noon the next day, when the ceremony was brought to a close and all joined in the feast. At this time the skin is told, "We will feed you again in two years."

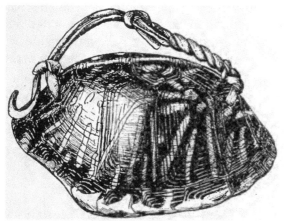

Fig. 18. - Rattle of land-tortoise shell used in the Otter Rite. (Length, 3.9 in.)

Buffalo Dance

Such was the list of native Lenape ceremonies furnished by our informants; but Adams [58] mentions several more, for which the writer was unable to procure much in the way of data. One of these was the Buffalo dance, which the writer feels should be included with the Otter and Bear ceremonies, although Adams calls it a "pleasure dance." He admits, it will be observed, that it usually took place before hunters started on the chase. His account follows:

"The Buffalo dance is a pleasure dance and always begins in the morning and lasts all day. The ground is made clean in a circle large enough to dance on, and in the center a tire is built and a fork driven into the ground on each side, and a pole placed across the fire east and west. On each side of the fire is a large brass kettle hanging across the pole with hominy in it, and when the dance is nearly over, the dancers eat the hominy, dipping their hands in the kettle. The singers are outside of the ring and beat on a dried deer hide stretched over poles. They do not use the same step in the dance, but gallop like buffaloes and bellow like them, also have horns on their heads and occasionally hook at each other. The dance is usually given before starting on a chase."

80

IMPORTED CEREMONIES

Skeleton Dance

The preceding ceremonies have all been, ostensibly at least, of native Lenape origin, but we now come to several whose outside origin is admitted by the Indians themselves. The most ancient of these is the "Human Skeleton Dance," mentioned by Adams. [59] He calls it a rite belonging to the Wolf clan or phratry of the Delawares, but the writer's informants say that it is not true Lenape at all, but a Nanticoke (One"ko) ceremony introduced among the Lenape by the survivors of that tribe who had joined forces with them. Adams' account, which is better than any the writer was able to obtain, is as follows:

"Human Skeleton Dance. — Given only by the Wolf clan of the Delawares. A certain dance given as a memorial to the dead was supposed to clear a way for the spirit of the deceased to the spirit land. When a member of the Wolf clan died, the flesh was stripped from the bones and buried, and the bones were dried at some private place. At the end of 12 days the skeleton would be wrapped in white buckskin and taken to a place prepared for the dance and there held up by some one. As the singers would sing the men who held the skeleton would shake it and the bones would rattle as the dancers would proceed around it. After the dance the skeleton was buried. Traditions say that in ancient times some of the head men in the Wolf clan had a dream that they must treat their dead in that way, and the custom has been handed down to them for many centuries. The other clans say the custom does not belong to them. The custom has been long dropped. There has not been a skeleton dance since 1860."

Fig. 19. — Peyote "Button." (Diameter, 1.9 in.)

The Peyote Rite among the Lenape
Native Painting by Earnest Spybuck, a Shawnee. (Plate IX.)

Peyote Rite

One of the latest of introduced ceremonies, which was still much in favor with the Oklahoma Lenape when last visited by the writer, is the Peyote Rite, a cult now widespread among the tribes of the Central West, introduced among this people by an Indian named John Wilson, who obtained it, they say, from the Caddo on Washita river about the year 1890 or 1892. During this ceremony remarkable visions are produced by eating the dried top of a small cactus, the peyote (fig. 19), for which the cult is named, and these visions, coupled with the moral teachings embodied in the ritual, make it very attractive to the Indian, who, on joining the cult, is often persuaded to discard entirely the ancient beliefs of his own people. The writer is acquainted with two principal forms of the rite, one involving native deities only, the other, almost entirely Christian in teaching and symbolism. It is this latter form which has been adopted by the Lenape, to whom the tipi, in which the ceremony is held, is as foreign an institution as the little cactus itself, brought in from southern Texas and Mexico.

Paraphernalia. — For this ceremony the tipi is erected with the door to the east, and a complex series of symbols arranged inside, as shown in the smaller drawing, pi. ix. On the western side of the lodge is built a crescent-shaped mound, or "moon," of earth, packed hard, its horns turned toward the east, which they say represents the tomb where Christ was buried, and on the center of this is placed a large peyote, dampened and flattened (fig. 19), resting either on a bed of feathers or on the bare earth; and to the west of this again, sometimes a crucifix, as shown in the illustration. Between the points of the crescent is built the fire in a certain prescribed manner with overlapping sticks forming an angle pointing westward. Near the door lies another mound — a round one representing the sun. From the peyote resting on the embankment to the sun mound, directly through the middle of the fire, a line is drawn in the earth of the floor. This represents the "peyote road" along which the Peyote Spirit takes the devotee on a journey toward the sun, and also symbolizes the road to Heaven that Jesus made for the souls of men when He returned thither. West of the crescent-shaped mound stands, when not in use, the highly decorated arrow or staff, frequently made in the form of a long cross, with a groove extending from end to end, representing the spirit road. A small water-drum made of a piece of deerskin stretched over a crock, as seen in pi. ix, a nicely carved drumstick, an eagle-feather fan for brushing all evil influence away from each devotee as he enters or leaves the ceremony, and a supply of dried peyote, dampened and crushed in a mortar, are all necessary for the ceremony. Each devotee, moreover, must be supplied with a decorated gourd rattle of his own.

Officers. — The only officers needed for this rite are a "Road-man" or speaker, who sits in the west, just opposite the door, and a fire guard stationed at the door, whose duty it is to keep the fire burning, and to brush with the feather fan the devotees as they enter. This is illustrated in the colored plate (pl. ix), which represents also the "Road-man" guiding a newcomer to a seat.

Conduct of the Ceremony. — When all are gathered in the tipi, the leader first passes around a fragment herb which the people chew and rub over hands and body. Then the macerated peyote is passed, and each takes enough to make eight pellets about half an inch in diameter, of which some eat all, some only part, reserving some pellets to be eaten later. About this time the leader addresses the peyote and the fire, prays, and often delivers a regular sermon or moral lecture. He then takes the staff in his left hand, and sitting, or kneeling on one knee, he sings a certain number of peyote songs, which are a class to themselves, while the man to the left beats the drum, then passes the staff to the person on his right, himself taking the drum while this person sings, and so the staff travels round and round the lodge, each taking his turn at singing, while the devotees, men and women alike, keep their eyes fixed upon the fire or upon the peyote lying on the mound. As the night wears on the "medicine" begins to take effect, and the devotees see many strange visions, pictures, and brilliant-colored patterns. Often one may see the Peyote Spirit, in the form of an old man, who takes his spirit on a wonderful journey along the "peyote road," eastward toward the sun. At daybreak they all file out of the tipi bearing their paraphernalia, as seen in pl. ix, b, and when the sun appears they raise their hands in salutation, and then those who are left standing (for some fall as if dead at the sight of the sun) "give thanks to the Great Father in Heaven." Those who fall at sunrise, they say, are the ones who visited the sun in their visions. All sleep, or at least rest, until about noon, when a feast is served, after which everyone tells what he or she saw while "on the peyote road."

The Lenape variant of this ceremony, as related above, differs somewhat from that of other tribes practising the Christian form of the Peyote rite, but in all essentials it is almost identical.

Ghost Dance

The Ghost dance was also introduced among the Lenape by an Indian named Wilson, about the same time, our informants thought, as the Peyote rite, and, like it, probably from the Washita River region.

Wilson would call a dance every now and then during his lifetime, at which the people appeared in their everyday dress, without such special costumes as were seen, for instance, at such functions among the Kiowa and the Arapaho. At these meetings the participants would dance round and round for a long time, with a sidewise step, to the sound of song and water-drum, sometimes for a considerable period without stopping. Occasionally one would fall and appear to faint, and when revived would claim to have visited Heaven in spirit while his body lay as if dead. When Wilson died, the cult, so far as the Delawares were concerned, perished with him.

Such were the ceremonies surviving until recent times among the Lenape, from which have been omitted only the observances connected with the dead, shamanism, witchcraft, and war, all of which will be discussed in later papers.

Chapter Nine - Summary religion

Study of the material presented shows that the Lenape believed in a Great Spirit, or Creator, whose goodness is acknowledged, who is thanked for past blessings and petitioned for their continuance, but who is not their only god. He is, however, the great chief of all, and dwells in the twelfth, or highest heaven. He created everything, either with his own hands or through agents sent by him, and all the powers of nature were assigned to their duties by his word. That these concepts are not new among the Lenape may be seen from the fact that most of the early writers who treat of this people have noticed such beliefs among them, which can be traced back as far as 1679.

This Great Spirit gave the four quarters of the earth and the winds that come from them to four powerful beings, or *manǐ'towǔk*, namely, Our Grandfather where daylight begins, Our Grandmother where it is warm, Our Grandfather where the sun goes down, and Our Grandfather where it is winter. To the Sun and the Moon, regarded as persons and addressed as Elder Brothers by the Indians, he gave the duty of providing light, and to our Elder Brothers the Thunders, man-like beings with wings, the task of watering the crops, and of protecting the people against the Great Horned Serpents and other water monsters. To the Living Solid Face, or Mask Being, was given charge of all the wild animals; to the Corn Spirit, control over all vegetation, while Our Mother, the Earth, received the task of carrying and feeding the people.

Besides these powerful personages were many lesser ones, such as the Small People, the Doll Being, the Snow Boy, and the Great Bear. Certain localities, moreover, were the abode of supernatural beings, while animals and plants were thought to have spirits of their own. Besides these there were, of course, the countless spirits of the human dead who were still supposed to retain some influence in earthly affairs.

This, then, was the supernatural world which, to the mind of the Lenape, controlled all things — on which they must depend for health, for success in all their undertakings, even the daily task of deer-hunting or corn-raising. Benevolent beings must be pleased, and bad spirits combated and overcome, or at least placated.

There was, however, until very lately, no conception of a "devil" in the modern sense of the word.

The main channel of communication between the supernatural world and man was the dream or vision, obtained, as before described, by fasting and consequent purification in youth. Through the vision the young man obtained his guardian spirit or supernatural helper, who gave him some power or blessing that was his main dependence through life, his aid in time of trouble, the secret of his success. No wonder, then, that visions and helpers form the basis of Lenape belief and worship. Among the guardian spirits figured not only such great powers as the Sun and the Thunder Beings, the personified powers of nature, but the spirits representing various species of animals and birds, such as the Wolf or the Owl, of plants, as "Mother Corn," as well as the Mask Being, and even the spirits of the dead which some Lenape claimed as helpers.

Those favored by such visions were considered the leading people of their community. They usually composed rythmic chants referring to their visions, and appropriate dance songs to go with them, to recite at the Annual Ceremony.

Belief in a soul or spirit surviving the death of the body formed an integral part of Lenape philosophy. The soul is supposed to linger for eleven days after death, and is addressed and offered food by the surviving relatives, sometimes in a formal "Feast of the Dead;" but on the twelfth day, they say, it leaves the earth and finally makes its way to the twelfth or highest heaven, the home of the Great Spirit, where it leads a happy life in a land where work and worry are unknown. Some persons are thought to have the power of communicating with the departed.

Ceremonies

Most of the beliefs summarized above were found among the descendants of both Unami and Minsi; but when we consider their great religious ceremonies, we begin to note differences. While it is true that (1) in both cases these rites are based on the recital of the visions seen by the participants, combined with thanksgiving to the Great Spirit and his helpers for past blessings and prayers for their renewal, that (2) the New Fire ceremony figures in both, and that (3) they take place in a building of special form and decoration erected for the purpose, we note that among the Unami the ceremony is conducted only once a year, and is combined to a certain extent with the cult of the *Misi'ngw'*, or Mask Being, a magnified guardian spirit or personal helper; while the Minsi have in addition to that held in the fall, a spring ceremony also, cognate with the Iroquois "Thanks for the First Fruits," or Strawberry Dance, and masked impersonators do not appear in the Minsi ceremonial house.

In the ceremonies of both Unami and Minsi, however, we note other similarities besides those first mentioned, such as the manner of prayer, the use of a drum made of a dried deer-hide beaten with flat forked drumsticks each bearing a carved face, the fumigation and sweeping of the Big House, the restriction against women in their menses, and the use of twelve as a sacred number.

It therefore seems likely that the rites, in spite of the differences noted, probably have a common origin, and hence (late back to a period before the separation of the Unami and the Minsi. Indeed we have an historical account which seems to refer to this kind of ceremony as early as 1683, while under date of 1779 there is a description of the rites practically as enacted as late as 1920.

Minor Ceremonies

Analyzing the minor ceremonies of Lenape origin we find the cults of two types: one founded on a beneficent spirit, a personal helper such as the Mask Being, whose relations are friendly with mankind; the other based on a discarded toy or pet, which makes trouble for its former owner unless propitiated by the ceremony in question.

A good example, in fact the only one we recorded, of the first type is the ceremony in honor of the Mĭsinghâli'kŭn, or Mask Being, among the Unami, which, however, does not find its counterpart among the Minsi, who had a Society of Masks whose rites and functions were similar to those of the Iroquois "False Face Company."

The second class embraces the cults of the Doll, Bear, and Otter, all of which must be propitiated periodically, under pain of sickness or death.

It will be observed that recitals of visions form a part of the Bear rites, and probably also of the Otter ceremony, all of which, taken into consideration with the preceding, gives rise to speculations concerning the basic form of Lenape ceremonies. Perhaps originally, everyone who had been blessed with a vision, held a periodic ceremony at which rites appropriate to his own guardian spirit were emphasized, but at which others so blessed could recite their own visions.

Of course ceremonies of extraneous origin, such as the Peyote rite, can not be classified with those of true Lenape origin; and there are others of which our accounts are so fragmentary that we can not place them, and still others, doubtless, that have disappeared entirely.

That such may have been the case is not remarkable — not nearly so extraordinary as the fact that the Lenape have retained so much of their ancient beliefs and practices after three centuries of contact with civilization.

Notes

[1] Handbook of American Indians, *Bulletin 30, Bureau of American Ethnology,* part I, p. 386, Washington, 1907. Indian Population in the United States and Alaska, 1910, p. 73, Washington, 1915. Annual Report of the Department of Indian Affairs for 1913, Ottawa, 1913.

[2] Dankers, Jaspar, and Sluyter, Peter. Journal of a Voyage to New York in 1679-80. Translated from the original manuscript in Dutch for the Long Island Historical Society, pp. 266-267, Brooklyn, 1869.

[3] Penn, William. A Letter from William Penn, Proprietary and Governour of Pennsylvania in America to the Committee of the Free Society of Traders of that Province, Residing in London, p. 6, London, 1683.

[4] Holm, Thomas Campanius. Short description of the Province of New Sweden, now called Pennsylvania. Mem. Hist. Soc. Pa., vol. in, p. 139, Phila., 1834.

[5] David Zeisberger's History of the Northern American Indians. Edited by Archer Butler Hulbert and William Nathaniel Schwarze. *Ohio Archaeological and Historical Quarterly,* vol. xix, nos. i and 2, p. 128, Columbus, 1910.

[6] Heckewelder, John. An Account of the History, Manners and Customs of the Indian Nations who once inhabited Pennsylvania and the neighboring States. *Transactions of the American Philosophical Society,* vol. 1, p. 205, Phila., 1819.

[7] Waubuno, *Chief* (John Wampum). The Traditions of the Delawares, as told by Chief Waubuno. London [n.d.]. This little pamphlet contains some original material on the Minsi and some purporting to appty to the Minsi, but copied from Peter Jones' "History of the Ojebway Indians."

[8] Brainerd, David. Memoirs of the Rev. David Brainerd, Missionary to the Indians...chiefly taken from his own diary, by Rev. Jonathan Edwards, including his Journal, now...incorporated with the rest of his diary ... by Sereno Edwards Dwight, pp. 344, 349, New Haven, 1822.

[9] Brinton, Daniel G. The Lenape and their Legends, p. 65 et seq., Phila., 1885.

[10] Loskiel, George Henry. History of the Mission of the United Brethren among the Indians in North America, p. 34, London, 1794. Zeisberger, op. cit., pp. 128-129. Heckewelder, op. cit., p. 205.

[11] Loskiel, op. cit.

[12] Zeisberger, op. cit., p. 130.

[13] Brainerd, op. cit., p. 238.

[14] Holm, op. cit., p. 139.

[15] Strachey, Wm. The Historie of Travaile into Virginia. *Hakluyt Soc. Pub.,* vol. vi, p. 98, London, 1849.

[16] Brainerd, op. cit., p. 344.

[17] Loskiel, op. cit., p. 43.

[18] Brainerd, op. cit.

[19] Loskiel, op. cit.

[20] Ibid.

[21] Ibid.

[22] Zeisberger, op. cit., p. 147.

[23] Heckewelder, op. cit., p. 205.

[24] Loskiel, op. cit., p. 43.

[25] Jones, Rev. Peter. History of the Ojebway Indians, p. 83, London, 1861.

[26] Skinner, Alanson, and Schrabisch, Max. A Preliminary Report of the Archaeological Survey of the State of New Jersey, *Bulletin 9 of the Geological Survey of New Jersey,* p. 32, Trenton, 1913

[27] Skinner, Alanson. The Lenape Indians of Staten Island, *Anthropological Papers of the American Museum of Natural History,* vol. in, p. 21, New York, 1909. Idem. Two Lenape Stone Masks from Pennsylvania and New Jersey, *Indian Notes and Monographs,* 1920.

[28] Brainerd, op. cit., p. 237.

[29] Zeisberger, op. cit., p. 141.

[30] Ibid., op. cit., p. 139.

[31] Brainerd, John, quoted by Abbott in Idols of the Delaware Indians, *American Naturalist,* Oct. 1882.

[32] Jones, op. cit., pp. 87, 95.

[33] Brainerd, David, op. cit., p. 344.

[34] Penn, William, op. cit.

[35] Brainerd, David, op. cit., p. 238.

[36] Ibid., p. 346.

[37] Zeisberger, op. cit., pp. 133-134.

[38] Ibid., p. 131.

[39] A similar vision of a black and white duck was reported by the Lenape at the Grand River reserve in Ontario. See Harrington, M. R., Vestiges of Material Culture among the Canadian Delawares, *American Anthropologist,* n.s., vol. x, no. 3, p. 414, July-Sept., 1908.

[40] Brainerd, David, op. cit., p. 347.

[41] Zeisberger, op. cit., p. 132.

[42] Loskiel, op. cit., p. 40.

[43] Heckewelder, op. cit., p. 238 et seq.

[44] Adams, R. C. Notes on Delaware Indians, in *Report on Indians Taxed and Indians not Taxed,* U. S. Census 1890, p. 299.

[45] Zeisberger, op. cit. p. 138.

[46] Ibid. pp. 136, 137.

[47] Harrington, M. R. A Preliminary Sketch of Lenape Culture, *American Anthropologist,* vol. xv, no. 2, April-June, 1913.

[48] Adams, loc. cit.

[49] Zeisberger, op. cit. p. 138.

[50] Harrington, Canadian Delawares, pp. 414, 415. See note 39.

[51] Waubuno, op. cit. p. 27.

[52] Brainerd, David, op. cit. p. 237.

[53] Adams, loc. cit.

[54] Harrington, Canadian Delawares, p. 416.

[55] Ibid. p. 417.

[56] Marsh, Rev. Cutting. Documents Relating to the Stockbridge Mission, 1825-48, *Wisconsin Historical Collections,* vol. xv, pp. 164-165.

[57] Zeisberger, op. cit. p. 138.

[58] Adams, loc. cit.

[59] Ibid.

Printed in the USA
CPSIA information can be obtained
at www.ICGtesting.com
LVHW091034090324
774009LV00002B/352